Get Your Swing in Gear

AuthorHouse™
1663 Liberty Drive
Bloomington, IN 47403
www.authorhouse.com
Phone: 1-800-839-8640

First published by AuthorHouse 12/21/09

ISBN: 978-1-4490-6384-9 (e)
ISBN: 978-1-4490-6383-2 (sc)
ISBN: 978-1-4490-6382-5 (hc)

Library of Congress Control Number: 2009913625

Printed in the United States of America
Bloomington, Indiana

This book is printed on acid-free paper.

Get Your Swing in Gear

Rob Bernard

authorHOUSE®

"A Premonition"

About the Author

Rob grew up in Eastern Canada on Prince Edward Island. Always a sportsman, Rob's first love was Hockey and his summer sport of choice was Tennis. Golf didn't come into the picture for Rob until his University years at the age of 22, but his fascination with the sport captured his full attention.

After turning Professional 15 years later this self taught player turned his full attention to developing and teaching his easy to learn, easy to remember, and easy to implement Center of Gravity Golf program. This overwhelmingly successful program has produced over 500 live seminars, entertaining and enlightening over 100,000 golfers, and has been taught in over 30 countries worldwide. The overwhelming response to the program resulted in this Book and DVD series "Get Your Swing in Gear".

You can contact Rob at **WWW.COGOLF.CA**

Dedication

I would like to dedicate this book to my Dad, *Gerard "Joe" Bernard*. A hall of fame athlete and man who was loved and respected by everyone who came in contact with him, not because of the speed of his fastball, how fast he could skate, or how hard he hit a golf ball... but for the man he was, every day of his life. Love you Dad...

Acknowledgements

There are many people I have to acknowledge who helped me get into a position to write this book.

Gladys Bernard: *(My Mom)* who raised 9 successful children and instilled in me, the confidence to succeed, every day, in any field of my choosing.

My brothers and sisters, who all had a hand in shaping my life and continue to support me on a daily basis,

Gail Moore
Pat Wick
Linda Hunter
Donna Peters
Paul Bernard
Susan Weatherbee
Greg Bernard
Heather MacLaurin

Joanne, my better half, who has lived this golf dream every day and continues to give me the support I need to build *Center of Gravity Golf* and help golfers everywhere *"Get Their Swing in Gear"*.

The Canadian Professional Golfers Association.
To all the dedicated members of the Canadian PGA who live to teach, promote, and grow the game of golf not only in Canada, but Worldwide.

Thank You...

Contents

Centre of Gravity Golf

Foreward:

After years of learning to play this great game followed by many years of teaching others to enjoy themselves on the golf course, I have concluded that golf instruction for the masses has been the communication of a complicated "mish-mash" of angles, gadgets, jargon, and contradictions, leaving the casual golfer confused... but wanting more. What I've done with Center of gravity Golf is break down the golf swing to a basic 1, 2, 3 motion that anyone can understand and implement. Understanding dynamic balance alone can help you be a more consistent swinger of the golf club and therefore a better ball striker. When put together in the proper sequence, the 1, 2, 3 golf swing will bring you many years of *frustration free*, golfing enjoyment.

I draw my philosophies on the golf swing from many expert sources such as Bobby Jones, David Lee, Harvey Pennick, David Pelz, & the great Canadian ball striker Moe Norman, just to name a few. While these great teachers and players of the game inspired me to be the best Golf Pro I could be, it was my Father, Gerard "Joe" Bernard, "an outstanding athlete in many sports", who taught me to break things down to their simplest form in order to really understand what was happening so I could work to improve quickly. So thanks Dad for that lesson, it stuck with me all these years. I believe I've accomplished what I set out to do with this book. If you're looking for complicated solutions with lots of jargon, references to Touring Professionals' golf swings, miracle gadgets to buy, or quick band-aid solutions, this is not the program for you. **C.O.G.** golf is an improvement program that is easy to understand, easy to implement, easy to remember, and it works. It is my goal that you improve today, so find a comfy spot and enjoy...

Rob Bernard Canadian PGA "Class "A"

1 "The Golf Swing Simplified"

What is C.O.G. Golf?

The **Center of Gravity Golf** system is a tool to learn, understand, and implement a golf swing that will produce more consistency in your ball striking, short game, and putting. No matter what your handicap is now, any time you reach a playing plateau where improvement is slow or non-existent, you are lacking in consistency in one or many parts of your game. When your consistency improves, your game improves along with your personal enjoyment level. I believe that personal enjoyment of the game is directly linked to the amount of frustration the player feels with each missed shot on a given hole. We all expect *(and can deal with)* a missed shot now and then, even the greatest players in the history of the game miss badly from time to time. It's the consistent miss hit that drives us to lose our cool and raises our frustration levels along with our scores.

The problem most of us have is that "Life" gets in the way of golf and we can't devote the time to practice or play as much as we would like. Taking lessons "I've found" is only effective if you can put into practice the ideas your Golf Pro is trying to instill in you as you try to remember exactly what you *thought* you heard at the lesson. As a Golf Professional, I can say the same thing, my job and life get in the way of practice time and play time so I had to develop a method to deal with the time constraints we all have, and **Center of Gravity Golf** was born. After years of teaching the old standard methods, and using a lot of trial and error, I combined the best of what actually worked with the **C.O.G.** golf method in order to accelerate the learning stages and create a high level of success quickly, which in turn increases player confidence and begins the cycle of improvement. I have experienced almost immediate success with virtually every player I've worked with using the **C.O.G.** methods, and I'm convinced it will work with you the same way no matter what level of golfer you currently are.

I have always felt golf guru Harvey Pennick was correct when he stated, *"If the student is not learning, the teacher is not teaching"*. I take personal responsibility if one of my students is not improving and does not have a greater knowledge of the cause and effect of the outcome of each shot he or she takes. Cutting through the jargon and technical speak to the point of understanding what's really happening is the key to learning and making positive changes to your game. This is the reason I have the policy to never accept payment for a lesson if significant improvement and understanding is not clearly evident by both the student and the teacher. The same goes for any video, book, or golf tip download purchased from our web site. *Communication,* "I feel", is the real key to learning and understanding and sometimes ideas and methods are lost or altered in translation or interpretation. For this reason, every word you read was written by me, in simple plain English and not an interpretation by a ghostwriter.

Frustrated?

Even though professional athletes from other sports consider golf to be the most difficult sport to play well, golfers all over the world, regardless of playing ability, have one thing in common...we all exhibit a level of frustration with the game. Whether you have trouble with your drives, fairway shots, chips, putts, or miss hits, the frustration level increases with each missed shot.

I don't think we get frustrated **because** we miss, after all, we are human...I think we get frustrated because we don't understand **why** we miss so we can work toward missing less. Let's face it...better players are better because they miss less. I'm sure you've heard the phrase, *"golf is a game of misses"*... and I believe truer words have never been spoken. Golf *is* a game of misses, and when we understand why we missed that last shot and can correct the mistake for next time, our frustration decreases and our confidence rises. Any time you have a decrease in frustration and a rise in confidence, your game (and your attitude) will improve.

Golf is truly a game that should be enjoyed at all levels of play regardless of score, and improving your consistency will alleviate some frustration and have you looking forward to the next game.

2 "The C.O.G. Golf Swing"

Where do you Start?

Let's start with equipment. I'm not going to get into your set make up or equipment brand, we can talk about that later, what I'm interested in at the moment are your grips. I don't care how good your equipment is, or how much it cost…if your grips are not in good shape, I *(or any Pro for that matter),* cannot properly teach you how to swing a golf club.

Almost everyone I come in contact with on the range or at the club takes pretty good care of his or her golf clubs, with the exception of the grips. The only contact you have with the golf ball is directly through the grips of your golf clubs, you have to take care of them. A Professional golfer has their grips cleaned after practice sessions, before a round, during a round, and has them changed regularly. Have you cleaned your grips yet? They should feel slightly tacky in your hands so you don't have to squeeze your golf club, which robs you of the ability to swing the golf club with any speed or consistency.

Most grips today are still made out of rubber or a rubber compound that can be kept in "like new" condition simply with hot soapy water. When you play golf or practice, the dust, dirt, and oil from your hands gets ground into the pores of the rubber, clogging them up and making your grips slick and hard. Washing your grips will clean out the pores making them feel tacky again and ready for your next round. If your grips have been neglected for a while, try a window cleaner solution on them, this will cut through the oils and dirt

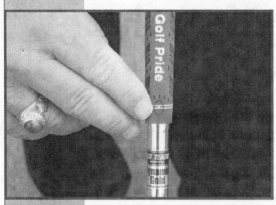

Figure 1
The Center
Mark of
Your Grip

and should bring even a neglected grip back to life. If they have been badly neglected and you can't get them back to a "tacky" state, have them replaced at your local Pro-Shop. The good news is they're very inexpensive, starting at around $2.00, and while you're there you can have them sized to fit your hand perfectly. This will help immensely when you learn to *swing* the golf club using the **C.O.G.** effortless power method.

OK, now that you've got your grips cleaned and looked after, keep them that way, like I said earlier, every Professional golfer has new grips or has their grips cleaned before every round. If you have a high tech grip material and you're not sure what to clean them with, simply contact the manufacturer and ask, they will last longer and perform much better.

Notice at the top and the bottom of your grip there is a small hash mark that indicates the center mark of your shaft. These are very important marks, take notice of them now, and we'll talk more about them later. Now that we have your grips looked after, we can talk about the *Boss* of the golf club.

The BOSS:

Your target side hand, *(the one with the glove)* is the *Boss* of the golf club, that's why we wear the glove on that hand. On the target hand, (the left hand for right handed golfers) *the top three fingers* assume control of the golf club. This is the *Pinky, the Ring, and the Middle finger*, leaving the index finger and thumb to rest lightly on the grip. When these three fingers are in control of the golf club, you will be able to swing the club at a high speed with very little effort and fire your *"Piston" (the act of releasing the club head)*.

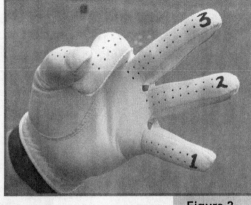

Figure 2
The Boss
Fingers

If your trail hand *(right hand for right hand golfers)* gets involved, it will slow down the swinging process and turn the action into a *"hit"*. Work on keeping the target hand the *Boss* of the club, this will help prevent two other common problems,

> **1) The hole in the glove…**
>
> **2) The "fat" shot…**

Hole in your glove?

> **3)** If you are the golfer that always has a hole in the heel of your golf glove, not only am I going to save you $50 to $100 dollars in golf gloves this year alone, but should save you quite a few strokes as well. The hole in your golf glove is a tell tale sign

Figure 3
Does your
glove look
like this?

that the *Boss* fingers are **giving up control of the golf club** when you take your back swing. At the top of your swing, when the *Boss* fingers let go, a **gap** is created between your fingers and the heel of your hand; the hole in the glove is soon to follow.

Figure 4
The Boss Fingers Letting Go creating the "GAP"

Why does this happen?

The head of a swinging golf club weighs about a pound for every mile per hour it moves through centrifugal force. A typical golf professional moves the club head from the address position to the top of the backswing in approximately 1 second. At the point of transition to the down swing, the club head weighs about 14 pounds. That's the equivalent of a 14-pound weight being held by the top 3 fingers of the target (gloved) hand.

Figure 5
Boss Fingers in Control, no gap

Most people can hold this weight OK but if the club travels to the top of the swing faster than that, the transition weight of the club head becomes heavier and the separation of the top 3 fingers (or the **GAP**) occurs. When the (**GAP**) happens, you transfer control of the club head to the Trail hand (right hand) and the butt end of the grip rubs or tears the leather of the glove on the transition to the downswing. This all happens very quickly and is hard to catch if you don't know what to look for or what is actually happening.

The dreaded hole in the glove is **NOT** a normal occurrence in golf; it is the product of a change of control of the golf club from your target hand to your trail hand during the course of transition from the top of your back swing to the beginning of your down swing. This action can and even **MUST** be controlled if you are to learn to swing a golf club like you see your favorite Professional swing it every day. We'll discuss how to control this a little later on in the book when we set up the easy 3-piece golf swing and discover that **1-move** can solve 4 problems we have in the backswing alone and set us up for consistency and power in our swing towards the target.

Another Benefit!

The other benefit of learning to control your golf club with the top 3 fingers of the *Boss* hand at the transition point to the downswing is controlling the "**FAT**" shot.

Figure 6
The Dreaded "Fat" shot

The fat shot is the one where you stick the club head into the ground before it touches the golf ball, sending it trickling mere feet from where you're standing. The fat shot is a totally wasted stroke as little or no ground is covered and we have to hit the same shot over again. At the transition point of your golf swing when the club changes direction back to the ball, if your *Boss* hand loses control of the golf club, the weight of the club head rests on the trigger finger (index finger) of your Trail hand (right hand) and that hand becomes the *Boss* of the golf club at that moment.

Once the trail hand becomes the *Boss* of the golf club, the down swing motion becomes too steep and your trail hand throws the club head into the ground behind the ball. If this is the case, you may have noticed your ball position creeping back in your stance and your shots traveling too low and too far for the club you're using at the moment. This is a side effect of a weak *Boss* hand; you have to change the geometry of your golf swing in order to make contact with the ball. When this condition develops, all kinds of mistakes can happen as you try to *judge* where the bottom of your swing is going to happen.

Always remember, when your target side hand *(the one with the glove)* is the *Boss* of the golf club, the bottom of your golf swing will always be on your **Center of Gravity** (shirt-button) so you can predict proper ball position, trajectory, and distance control of each club in your bag, and eliminate the dreaded *FAT* shot.

What about the other Hand?:

What is the role of the trail hand on the golf club? I have found that the Trail hand *(right hand for right handed players)* plays the role of balancing the golf club, keeping the golf swing on plane *(by guiding the club to the top of the swing)*, and keeping the golf swing "together". The Trail hand therefore plays a very important part in the accurate delivery of the club head to the ball. I think the more important issue is what it **doesn't** do in the golf swing. Let's make a list…

1) The Trail Hand does **not** pull the golf club to the top of the swing.

2) The Trail Hand does **not** initiate the downswing at the transition point.

3) The Trail hand is **not** the *Boss* of the golf club at any point during the swing.

More golf swings are ruined before they start from an over active trail hand on the golf club. The moment the trail hand becomes the *Boss* of the golf club it can affect a number of important aspects of a good swing.

1) It can shorten the *"arc"* of the swing causing a *"too steep"* downswing that robs power and consistency.

2) It can alter *your* natural swing *"plane"* by pulling the club too far inside or too upright causing erratic results.

3) It can alter your swing *"Pace"* by getting the club to the top of the swing too fast, adversely affecting balance and control of the golf club.

4) It can alter or completely negate your *"Turn"* away from the ball so you do not "Prime" your *Engine*, causing an all arms swing that is not powerful.

5) It **will** cause fat shots (hitting behind the ball) by throwing the club head down into the dirt during the swing transition.

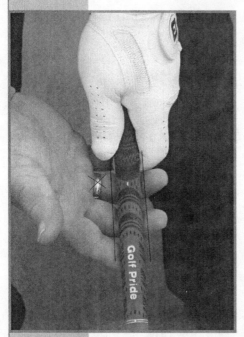

All of the issues described above can be avoided by simply allowing the top 3 fingers of the Target hand to remain the *Boss* of the golf club throughout the swing motion.

When you grip the golf club, run the grip across the center joints of the fingers of your trail hand, this prevents it from applying too much pressure to the grip. I always wear my PGA ring on my right hand as a reminder to keep the grip in the fingers. I never let the grip

Figure 7
The grip runs cross the center joints of the trailing hand fingers, never touching my ring

of the golf club   to touch my ring, keeping the ring round, while allowing my left hand to keep control of the club.

Interlock, or Overlap?

The connection of the two hands on the golf club is vital in order to have control and allow the hands to work as one unit; however the question of how a player should connect the hands is almost always uncertain.

I think that the proper connection of the hands depends on the length of the fingers and the comfort level when holding the club. The two most popular connections are the Overlap, or Vardon grip, made popular by Henry Vardon, and the Interlock grip, popularized by players such as the great Jack Nicklaus. In the Overlap grip, the pinky of the trail hand simply rests on top of the gap between the index and middle fingers of the target hand. In the Interlock grip, the pinky finger of the trail hand interlocks between the index finger and the middle finger of the target hand.

I believe most modern players prefer the Vardon, or overlapping grip as it allows the club to stay in the fingers of the trail hand more easily. In order for me to use the interlocking connection, I have to put the golf club into the base of the fingers of my right hand, and as I stated before, I don't allow the grip to touch my ring, so I must keep it in the center joints of the fingers. If you have long fingers, the interlocking connection may feel and work the best for you. When you come right down to it, it's a personal preference and you should try both, keeping in mind the grip should stay in the fingers of the trail hand.

If neither of these combinations feels comfortable, you can try the 10-finger grip. With this grip, all 10 fingers are on the grip and there is no connection of the hands aside from touching. The trouble with the 10 finger grip is the ease in which the trail hand can assume control of the golf club at the transition point. Having said this, it may be the best for you if your hands are not strong and you need the extra leverage in order to control the golf club.

Now that we understand the *Boss* of the golf club, let's have a look at how to create consistency in your golf game.

Figure 8
The Interlock
Grip

Figure 9
The Overlap
Grip (Vardon)

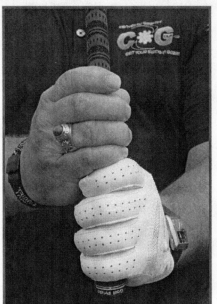

Figure 10
The Ten Finger
Grip

3 " The Secret to Golf"

The Secret to Golf?

If you open a golf magazine or turn on the golf channel, chances are you're going to run across somebody that claims to have the "Secret" to a more consistent golf game. Ben Hogan said the secret to golf was in the dirt; I think he just meant practice until you get it right. Others have wonder gadgets and widgets that they claim will make you a consistent ball striker or a more powerful player. There are believers in "swing plane", "weight transfer", shoulder turn", "strong grips", "weak grips", or whatever, some even think the answer is in new equipment.

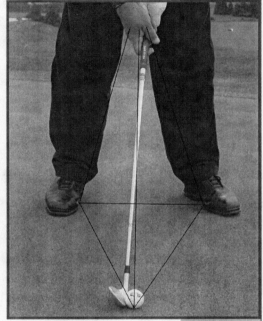

Figure 11
The Center of Gravity Triangle

While all of these things certainly have a place in golf, and maybe in your golf swing, none of them should be considered *the* "Secret" to the game. This is because there's a common denominator that *must* be under control for any of the aforementioned fixes to work at all. In my opinion, if there is a "secret to golf" it has to be what I call the *Center of Gravity Consistency Triangle*. In order for your golf club to find the bottom of your swing on a regular basis, the consistency triangle (*which runs from your Center of Gravity, to the knuckles of your big toes, and back to the golf ball*) has got to stay intact. Any time your center of gravity triangle moves, the bottom of your swing moves with it. Since the ball doesn't move around with the triangle, you miss, no matter how pretty or on plane your swing was.

Let's talk about the consistency triangle, what it consists of, and how to control it so you can learn to become a consistent golfer more quickly.

Understanding C.O.G. for Consistency:

Being a consistent ball striker, or increasing your consistency on the golf course, really begins with an understanding of the geometry of the golf swing and how to control it. I believe the golf swing is simple geometry and physics. Understanding this geometry and how the physics of the swinging motion tries to alter it is the key to becoming a consistent ball striker.

I was always taught that the triangle running across your chest to your shoulders and down your arms to the grip of the golf club was the triangle you had to maintain in order to create or maintain consistency in your ball striking. What I've discovered through the *Center of Gravity* golf method is that the above described triangle does NOT control consistency in ball striking, and actually impedes the natural flow of the golf swing by trying to consciously control it. The real consistency triangle you **must maintain** throughout the swinging process runs from your Center of Gravity (*use your shirt button as a reference* *point)*, to the knuckles of your big toes, *(where the bunions grow)* and back to the golf ball. This triangle formed at the address position must be maintained through the impact position in order to create a consistent bottom or impact point to your swing.

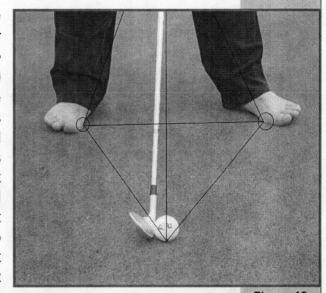

Figure 12
The knuckles of your Big Toes are your anchors

When your **target hand** is allowed to be the *Boss* of the golf club, the bottom of your swing will always be where your center of gravity is. If you move your C.O.G. sideways, backwards, or forwards during the downswing, you've changed the geometry of your triangle and the bottom of your swing has changed. One of the nice things about golf is that the ball never moves until you move it. On the other hand, if your C.O.G. is always moving, the ball doesn't move with you, causing a miss hit. This is usually the point where golfers start making changes or alterations in their golf swing or ball position to compensate for the miss-hits, which only complicates the geometry of the swing further, creating longer lasting problems.

And thus begins the life cycle of the frustrated golfer. Frustration comes from making the same mistake over and over and not understanding why. When you learn to control your consistency triangle, you WILL become a more consistent ball striker and your frustration levels WILL drop allowing you to have more fun on the golf course, while enabling you to concentrate more on your scoring game. We'll get to that a little later on. So how do you control this consistency triangle? Let's have a look.

Figure 13
The C.O.G. triangle moved the bottom of the swing backwards, result, thin miss. (topped shot)

Figure 14
The C.O.G. triangle moved the bottom of the swing sideways, result, thin miss. (topped shot)

4 "Controlling your C.O.G."

Get Control of your Feet:

While there are a few things we can do to help control our consistency triangle, the number one thing you can do **today** is to get control of your feet.

I've played a lot of sports in my day; hockey, football, tennis, baseball, among others, some at a very high level, and they all have one thing in common.

Figure 15
Feet are in Control of the Ground

I don't know of any sport you can play successfully from your heels, golf included. If you've played any other sports you'll understand what I mean. If golf is your first, or only sport so far, listen up because this will change everything.

First of all allow me to clear something up, if you play golf, you are an athlete, don't let anyone tell you anything different. Golfers put their body through tremendous athletic stress during a full and powerful golf swing, maxing out power in many muscle groups

Figure 16
Feeling "weak" at the top of the swing, the anchor lost control of the ground causing my triangle to move out of place

at the moment of impact. Athletes all have something in common; they know how to control their dynamic balance *(balance while in motion)*. Golfers not only have to control the dynamic balance of their body turn in order to maintain their consistency triangle, they have to do it while swinging an object around their C.O.G. which is trying to pull them off balance. The faster the object swings, the more it tries to pull you off balance. This is the reason golfing athletes have to understand how dynamic motion affects their C.O.G. and that they must learn how to control it or forever suffer the frustration of the miss-hit golf shot.

Stay off your Heels:

In athletic speak, being weak, caught off guard, or caught flat-footed, all mean the same thing; being caught off balance. Players in any sport get beat, manhandled, scored on, drop balls, or miss shots when they are caught off balance. When your weight shifts from the "strong" balance points of your feet to the "weak" off balance points of your heels, is when you lose control of the situation, and the situation controls you.

This is very true of golf as well, however, the beauty of golf is there are no other players taking advantage of your off balance moment to capitalize on your weakness. You and you alone are totally in control of your balance and have lots of time to set your shot up without the fear of another player knocking you about.

Figure 17
Weight on the heels, a weak athletic position

As I walk down the line of any driving range, more than 90% of the golfers are in their set up position with the majority of their weight towards the heels of their feet. This is **NOT** a strong athletic position. I know this because a small touch on their shoulder as I walk past sends them reeling backwards trying not to fall down. In order to be an athletic golfer, you **MUST** feel strong at the address position. Learn to manage your balance points by pressing the knuckles of your big toes into the ground; they are the *Boss* of the ground. The knuckles of your big toes are your anchors and should be in full contact with the ground and the heaviest points on your feet at the address position. I am **NOT** saying be on your toes, do not go onto your toes, in fact, if you want to feel these spots, curl your toes up, and press your knuckles into the ground. Now that you are in a strong address position, an athletic position, feel how in control you are.

The next important position and probably the MOST important for maintaining your consistency triangle and balance is the top of your swing. You have to feel strong at the TOP of your swing as well. This is the position where the club head and the turning of your body try to pull your balance points off the knuckles of your big toes and redistribute it towards your heels. Don't let it! If the balance points of your feet change mid-swing, your geometry will change, your consistency triangle is out of shape, and if you don't make precise adjustments on your downswing, you will miss.

So why do most golfers try to play this game from their heels? I think for the most part they are not aware of what their feet are doing during the swing *(it happens very fast).* Another reason I believe is the cause of most miss hit shots, and continued grief on the golf course, are these four little words...

5 "Keep your Head Down?"

I'd like to know who coined the phrase "Keep your head down" or "You lifted your head". This phrase has become the mantra for almost every golfer I've ever seen or heard miss a golf shot. "I must have lifted my head" are the first words out of a golfers mouth when a shot goes bad, and of course there's always the ever helpful playing partner who's quick to give that everlasting, cure-all advice "you lifted your head". This phrase (in my opinion) has caused, and will continue to cause, miss-hit golf shots until players understand you can't keep your head down

Figure 18
Head down causes swing balance problems

and stay in balance. Whenever a player misses a shot and a friend tells him he lifted his head, the player buries his chin in his chest so as to be sure not to lift his head again. This action sets in motion a series of events during the swing that are almost guaranteed to adjust your consistency triangle mid swing.

This is what Happens:

Your head weighs between 12 to 15 lbs, when you put your chin in your chest, that's up to a 15 pound weight pulling you toward your toes. At the address position, you can easily hold your balance points on the knuckles of your big toes while you're stationary, but the moment you move the club head away from the ball, you have a 12-15 pound weight moving around your body (the swinging club head), and a 12 –15 pound weight pulling you towards your toes (your head). Your Central Nervous System (CNS) then takes over; it's the body's natural defense mechanism that will not allow you to fall on your face in front of your friends on Saturday morning. The moment you begin to fall forward, your CNS readjusts your weight distribution back to the heels of your feet. This keeps you upright throughout your swing, but your consistency triangle is way out of shape and the bottom of your swing has changed, causing you to miss hit the shot.

Figure 19
Head down causes weight to shift backwards at the top of the swing

Always remember to keep your chin up and off your chest, (like you are holding a grapefruit under your chin). This will ensure your move away from the ball won't result in an off balance swing.

Do You Wear Glasses?

You may not realize this, but bi-focal lenses, tri-focal lenses, even gradient power lenses will cause you to have an off balance swing time after time. In order for you to see the ball, you must put your chin in your chest to see through the distance portion of your lens. With your chin in your chest, the off balance cycle continues, every swing.

Have a pair of golfing glasses made with only your distance lens. Make sure they have a nice size frame so you can keep your chin up and still see through the bottom of the lens. This could be the best piece of golf equipment you ever had, and it will improve your dynamic balance immediately.

Figure 20
Chin Up equals good balance

Iron Byron:

If you want to see the consistency triangle in action you need look no further than the "Iron Byron" golf ball-hitting machine developed by the True Temper Company to test shafts.

Iron Byron is commonly used by the USGA to test golf equipment and golf balls for conformity and performance. They can make Iron Byron hit the middle of the clubface, the toe of the club, the heel of the club, virtually anywhere they want. Iron Byron never misses.

The reason this machine is so reliable revolves around its consistency triangle. Iron Byron's feet are bolted to the floor, its center of gravity cannot move backwards, forwards, or sideways during the golf swing, all it can do is move round and round from its pivot point keeping its C.O.G. triangle intact. If we understand how consistency is attained by this machine, we can learn how to create and control our own consistency triangle and enjoy golf with less miss hit shots.

Getting your Swing Started:

Once you've set up the ball and committed to your club selection and target, getting your swing started properly will set you up for success, while a poor take away or backswing can have devastating consequences on the outcome of the shot. Learning to place the golf club in the proper position at the top of your swing is easier than you might think, once you know how, and with the sequence of good things that happen automatically, you'll be setting yourself up for a powerful swing time after time. As we talked about earlier, the C.O.G. swing method is broken down into 3 easy steps, the first of which is the *Push*.

6

Getting the Swing Started
"The Push"

Learning the 1...2...3... Golf Swing

Step 1, The Push

With the top 3 fingers of your left hand firmly in charge of the golf club, you have to push the handle of the golf club away from the ball in order to create a wide, on plane, powerful swing. In fact, the *Push* away from the ball takes care of 4 things I know you've read about and have probably fretted over once or twice during a round.

1) **ARC size or WIDTH:** The *Push* away from the golf ball takes care of the **arc** size or **width** of your swing. The arc of a golf swing is simply the size of the circle the club head makes as it swings around your body. The wider the arc, the more powerful the swing. When you push the handle of the golf club away from the ball and keep your *Boss* hand away from your head, (don't collapse your arms) your Arc size, or width, is maximized and you have established potential for full power.

2) **PACE:** The pace of the back swing, or the time it takes for the golf club to reach the top of your swing, is critical in maintaining dynamic balance during your swing as well as keeping control of the club with your *Boss* hand. The pace or time of the back swing should be around 1 second in order for a player to maintain these variables and have control over the swing. When the

Boss fingers are allowed to push the handle to the top of the swing, the pace slows to around 1 second allowing you to deliver the club back to the ball powerfully, in balance, and in control of the golf club.

Figure 21
Simply push the handle of the club away from the ball to control 4 things

3) PLANE: "Swing Plane" is a term that has been talked about at infinitum and usually confuses the casual golfer causing undue stress and too much to think about. The swing plane is nothing more than the angle the golf club swings around your body. A croquet mallet between your legs swings at 90º and a golf club swung from the side swings at an angle less than 90º. The length of the club as well as the build and physical limitations of the person holding it determine the angle or "plane" of the backswing. Therefore there is no perfect swing plane for every golfer. If you push the handle of your golf club away from the ball, keeping your *Boss* hand away from your head, (not collapsing your arms) you will push it on your swing plane, (should be at or near your shoulder line). Now forget about swing plane... you have it handled.

4) TURN: Your turn away from the golf ball is important for creating power by priming your *Engine*. The *Engine* of the golf swing is the primary rotation of the swing and must be primed up on the backswing or you will end up having an all arms swing that does not create effortless power. By pushing the handle of the golf club away from the ball, you prime up your *Engine* and force the body's weight to shift to the inside of your right foot *(knuckle of your big toe)*. Once your *Engine* is primed, you are ready to swing the golf club with effortless power.

Simply pushing the handle of the golf club away from the ball will take care of all these things that you will never have to worry, or think, about again. The goal of the Center of Gravity golf system is to simplify the golf swing so you have less to think about and can swing the club freely to your target. Now that we have part 1 taken care of, let's talk about part 2 of the 3-part golf swing, the **Engine.**

Notes:

7 "The Engine"

Golf is a Rotational Sport:

The first thing we must understand if we are going to learn to swing the golf club effortlessly and powerfully is that golf is a rotational sport, not a hitting sport. When I first picked up a golf club and stared down at that little white ball, I wanted to hit it with every fiber of my being. I know you've felt the same urge from time to time, perhaps every time you stand over a golf ball. I think this urge to hit is born into us and is almost instinctual, however, learning to resist the "hit" and simply swing the golf club will change the way you look at, and play, the game forever.

"Over the Top", "Right side dominant", steep swing angle, and chopping at the ball, are all caused by our overwhelming desire to HIT the ball. Learning the 3 piece golf swing will allow you to swing the golf club the way it was intended, powerfully, effortlessly, and accurately.

There are 2 rotations in the golf swing since there has to be two in order to make the golf ball go straight, but we'll get into that later. The first rotation in the golf swing, I call the "*Engine*".

Do all your Clubs go the same distance?

One of the biggest complaints I get from students is that all their clubs travel the same distance. It makes no difference what club they use, 5 iron, 7 iron, 6 iron, they all seem to go the same distance. If this sounds familiar to you, read on. When all your clubs go the same distance I call this having a (1...1...) golf swing.

A (1...1...) golf swing has no distinction between the 3 parts of the golf swing, and everything goes a very predictable, short distance.

While this swing is very useful around the greens, it's not very useful on the fairways and tee boxes. The full, effortless power golf swing requires 2 distinct rotations that we're going to learn about right now. We'll talk about the (1...1...) swing later when you need it... and you will need it.

Step 2, The Engine, the Primary Power Source:

The primary rotation of the golf swing is what I call the *Engine*. The *Engine* of the swing is the turning of the belt buckle from a position behind the golf ball at the top of your swing, to your intended target. Why behind the golf ball? Because when you use the *Push* we talked about earlier to start the golf swing, you prime the *Engine* by turning your belt buckle behind the position of the ball.

It is now the *Engine's* turn to start the downswing by turning towards the target. The turn of the *Engine*, I feel, has been made complicated by phrases like "Lateral Shift", "Clearing of the hips", and "Shifting of the weight". These phrases indicate you must do something other that simply turn your belt buckle to the target. If you try to laterally shift your weight by bumping your hip, or consciously shifting your weight to your left side, you effectively lock up your *Engine* and produce an all arms swing.

Weight shift in the golf swing is a round and round motion, not a side-to-side motion. The side-to-side move changes the bottom of your swing, causing inconsistency; round and round keeps your center of gravity on the ball, leading to greater consistency in your golf game. The *Engine* is an important component of the golf swing in more ways than one.

1) Your *Engine* is primed up by the pushing of the golf club to the top of the swing by the *Boss* fingers of the target side hand (the one with the glove).

Figure 22
The Engine in front of the club-head at impact, this creates "lag"

2) Your *Engine* initiates the golf swing from the transition point at the top of your swing.

3) Your *Engine* is the first rotation that produces the (Effortless Power) swing we all hear about.

4) Turning your *Engine* first allows you to synchronize the two rotations of the golf swing, producing powerful, straight shots and creates club head "lag". Your *Engine* consists of the core muscles of the abdominal region that turn and stabilize your body during the golf swing. The "turn" is really a very simple move, here are the steps.

Figure 23
Engine
doing its
job, triangle
intact

4.1) Stand with your feet shoulder width apart. If your stance is too wide, it is very hard to complete your turn to the target.

4.2) With your hands on your hips, simply turn your belt buckle to the target and roll up on the toe of your trail foot. If you turn and show me the whole bottom of your trail foot, your *Engine* will have gotten its job done (faces the target). Another way to say it is to turn your belt buckle to the target and roll up on your toe until your right knee touches your left knee. Whatever visual queue you need to get the job done properly is OK…as long as you don't stall your *Engine* (stop it short of the target).

Don't Stall Your Engine:

One of the most common swing faults, I believe, is the stalling of the *Engine*. Your *Engine* stalls when it stops rotating toward the target and your arms fly past the bottom of your swing before it can get its job done.

The "All arms swing", the "Over the top swing" and the "Hit from the Top swing" are all caused by a stalled *Engine*. If your *Engine* gets its job done you can't swing "over the top", as this is caused by a stalled *Engine*, which causes a reverse in the rotation sequence, which we will discuss a little later.

Take notice of any professional golfers' impact position on a full shot. When the club head reaches the bottom of the swing, the *Engine* (belt buckle)

Figure 24
A Stalled Engine = all arms swing

has passed the bottom of the swing, pulling the golf club into the "Slot". It's the *Engine* that pulls the golf club into the slot and creates the club head's proper path to the target, while generating the initial power you need to create consistent distance on every swing. When we learn and understand the importance of the *Engine* in the golf swing in both your long game and your short game, we'll start to give it more attention and let it do the job. Learning the simple "turn" method we described earlier and understanding that this "turn" is the *Engine* of the swing will set you on your way to consistency and distance you may have never experienced before.

Notes:

8 "The Piston"

Step 3, The Piston:

The second rotation you need to complete your golf swing is a rotation I call the *Piston*. The *Piston* is the compression rotation of the swing, the one that crushes the golf ball and makes it fly.

The modern golf ball is the most regulated piece of equipment we have today. Even in the times of drivers with exotic shaft materials and moveable weights, the golf ball continues to be the most advanced. Golf Balls are packed with energy and a Professional golfer knows how to get the energy out of the ball... by compressing it.

Figure 25
Wrists "Flipping" no release, weak, high shot

Figure 26
Piston firing, powerful release. Strong, spinning shot

Compressing a golf ball simply means squeezing it against the clubface and maximizing the rebounding properties of the ball. This results in increased ball speed, and increased spin rate, resulting in maximum carry distance for the particular club used.

I always ask my students if they've ever heard of the term *"releasing the club head"*. Almost 100 % of people I ask have heard the term from a Pro, from an article they've read, or from the Golf Channel, and agree that it's a very important part of the golf swing, but when I ask them if they can explain it to me, almost 100% of them have no idea what it is.

The *Piston* rotation is the compression move that squeezes the golf ball and creates long and straight shots. This is the move that is described as *"releasing the club"*. It's been called many things such as supination and pronation, releasing the club head, and flipping or rolling the wrists, but what actually happens is a natural rotation of the left forearm through the bottom of the swing, providing your *Piston* is engaged and ready to fire.

Figure 27 Neutral grip allows complete 90 degree rotation of the club head

Engaging Your Piston:

Engaging your *Piston* is simply the act of gripping the golf club with your target hand (the one with the glove) in such a way that your arm is hanging naturally and your forearm will rotate the toe of the golf club 90 degrees to the ball when turned. When this can happen without forcing the issue, your *Piston* is engaged. Most of the golfers I work with have a disengaged *Piston* and therefore have only 1 rotation, which results in short ball flight and directional problems.

In order to engage your *Piston*, simply take your address position and allow your arms to hang naturally. This natural relaxed position of your arms and hands translates into a "neutral" grip on the golf club allowing a full 90-degree rotation of the toe of the club to the golf ball. If the toe of the club under rotates (less than 90 degrees), your grip is deemed to be "weak", and if the toe of the club over rotates, (more than 90 degrees) it is deemed to be "strong".

Figure 28
Weak grip does not allow complete rotation of club head

A weak grip on the club (under rotates) will cause the golf ball to start off right of the intended target, while a "strong" grip on the club (over rotates) will cause the ball to start left of the target when you synchronize the *Engine/Piston* rotations of the golf swing. When your grip is neutral, (a 90 degree rotation) the ball will start off at the intended target when you synchronize the *Engine/Piston* rotations.

Figure 29
Mark your neutral grip position

Find the Mark on the Grip:

We talked about the golf grip earlier in the book when we agreed it should always be kept clean and changed when worn and slick. If the grip is not good, we cannot swing the golf club and have to resort to a hitting motion.

When you clean your grips, look for a small vertical hash mark at the top and bottom of the grip, sometimes they're barley visible. These are the centering marks for the grip and should run straight down the center of the shaft. When these marks are lined up, the leading edge of the golf club is square to your target line.

Once you have your Power Arrow marked on your glove, simply point the arrow at the bottom hash mark and your *Piston* will be engaged and ready to fire

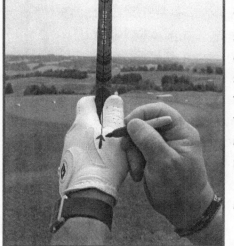

every time. If for some reason your grips don't have this mark, simply mark the shaft of your club at the bottom of the grip so you have a reference point for your Power Arrow. This visual queue will make sure you always set your *Piston* in the power position.

Mark Your Power Arrow:

Figure 30
Mark your "Power Arrow" to point to the center mark on grip

Some people find it difficult to break the habit of weakening their grip with the target hand by turning the hand under the grip, placing the thumb on top of the grip and effectively disengaging the *Piston*. When you find the spot where your *Piston* is engaged, mark your glove with your "Power Arrow".

The Power Arrow will remind you every time you grip the club to make sure your *Piston* is engaged before you begin your swing. To mark your Power Arrow, simply find your neutral power grip and mark an arrow on your glove that points to the Center hash mark or center logo on the club's grip. These hash marks or logos should run straight down the middle of the shaft, ensuring a proper power grip set up every time. I mark the Power Arrow on all my students' gloves as it gives them an edge until it becomes second nature. Follow the picture instructions and mark yours now.

Firing the Piston:

If you are tired of slicing the golf ball or pushing all your shots to the right, this is going to change your golfing life. If you fire your *Piston* on time during your swing, there is no chance the ball can go to the right. The firing of the *Piston* compresses the golf ball and sends it off the golf club on line to the target. I believe when you learn to fire your *Piston* on time you will take the right side of the golf course out of play. The firing of the *Piston* is a simple 90 degree rotation of the toe of the golf club with the left forearm through the hitting area.

Figure 31
When the *Piston* fires, the toe of the club points up after impact

The good news is, when your Power Arrow is set, the arm is designed to rotate at the bottom of

Figure 32
When the
Piston
ceases,
you get the
"Chicken
Wing" and
the club face
stays open

the swing if you let it. It is the natural rotation of the forearm and will fire on its own if you don't consciously hold it, or *cease* it. The problem with most of us is that we cease our *Piston* and don't allow it to fire.

Do you Cease your Piston?

The ceasing of the *Piston* is a very common occurrence in many golf swings. I can remember learning once that we have to hold the clubface square to the target line as long as possible. If we try to hold the clubface square to the target line, we lose the second rotation of the golf swing. This common piece of advice has caused more ceased *Pistons* and slices than I'd care to count.

Have you ever heard of the "Chicken Wing"? This is a term to describe the pushing out of the left elbow as the golf club moves down the target line. A ceased *Piston* causes the "Chicken Wing". If the *Piston* does not fire through the bottom of the swing, you get a "Chicken Wing"…fire the *Piston*, no "Chicken Wing", period. You cannot hold the clubface square to the target line, you must allow the second rotation to happen in order to release the club head and compress the golf ball. Compressing the golf ball will also help give you the desired ball flight that is not only longer, but also peaks later and will hold greens.

Ball Flight:

Ball flight is not something most golfers think about very much but it sure means a lot to the players who earn a living playing this game. Controlling your ball flight allows you to accurately predict distance and hold the greens when the ball lands.

The line above shows a typical ball flight of most golfers. You will notice the rainbow shape of the flight where the apex of the flight is half way between where the ball started, and where it landed. This is the flight of a ball that has been "pushed" to the target and when it lands it continues to roll out. This is the ball that hits in the middle of the green and then rolls into the bunker or into the rough at the back of the green. This flight will not hold the green so you must land the ball short and let it run up to the green. This is the typical ball flight of a golfer that has not fired their *Piston*. Remember we said that firing your *Piston* compresses the golf ball creating greater initial velocity and a higher spin rate, allowing the aerodynamic properties of the golf ball take over so it can *fly*.

The line below shows the typical ball flight of a golf ball that has been compressed.

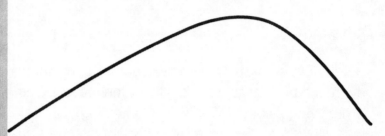

This ball flight apex is much higher and much closer to the intended target, allowing it to come to rest on the putting surface and stay put. Now you have the opportunity to make a birdie or par putt and not have to chip the ball back onto the putting surface from the back of the green. This is the typical ball flight of the golfer that fires their *Piston*, compressing the ball and making it *fly* by using the built in power of the golf ball. By learning to fire your *Piston*, you have the slice under control, and you can hold the greens as well…nice bonus.

Figure 33
The modern Golf Ball is the most powerful piece of golf equipment you can buy

The Golf Ball:

One thing most golfers never think about is the golf ball they're playing with. The modern golf ball is the most regulated piece of golf equipment we have today. Even with the new driver technology, exotic shaft material, and high rebound clubfaces of the most modern irons, the golf ball is still the most advanced of them all.

There has been a proposal put forth to golf's governing bodies to standardize the modern ball for Professional play to even the playing field. Of course I don't believe this will ever happen given the billions of dollars spent of brand specific golf balls and the personal preferences of the players. I can remember not long ago we only had 2 or 3 golf balls to choose from. We had the "red" numbered 90-compression ball and the "black" numbered 100-compression ball. It was known then that the 90-compression ball was for Ladies and slow swingers, and the 100-compression ball was for Pros and hard hitters.

With today's technology, the most popular golf ball in the world for Pros and top Amateurs is one that's compression runs in the mid 70s. This is quite a difference, especially when the 90-compression ball was considered to be for Ladies and slow club head speeds. Every major golf ball manufacturer today has an offering in the low compression ball market and the segment is growing fast. These are anywhere from 50 to 60–compression and down as low as 40 in a few. These golf balls are designed to fly farther with slower swing speeds because the golfer can compress the ball more easily and use the energy not only from the club head, but also all the energy packed into the ball. This new technology golf ball can be found in all pro-shops from virtually every ball manufacturer. Try one out, when you fire your Engine and *Piston*, you WILL see and feel a difference.

Notes:

9 "Synchronizing your Swing"

Synchronizing your Swing is the Key:

Synchronizing of the golf swing is the key to enjoying long, soaring golf shots that go to your intended target. The proper sequence of the golf swing is what I describe as the **1...2...3...**golf swing, or *Push...Engine...Piston*. When the golf swing occurs in this order, you produce the effortless power swing you see your favorite Professional using all the time. The synchronization of the golf swing is the key to getting the ball to go where you want it to go by keeping the golf club in the "slot" (turning the engine) and releasing the club head to the target (*Piston*). Remember, the *Push* takes care of "Pace", "Arc", "Plane" and "Turn" and sets up the top of the swing position for proper unwinding of the golf swing from the bottom, up.

The most common golf swing sequence I see on the golf course and at the range is the **1...3...2...** swing. This happens when you start the (upper body) rotation before the (engine) rotation, and you get the *"over the top", "all arms", "chopping wood", or "casting the club"* type of swing. If all your divots point to the left, you have a **1...3...2...**golf swing. Once you push the handle of the golf club to the top of the swing and feel in balance, you are set up for a good golf swing if you can re-program the sequence to fire the engine first. When you fire the engine first, you cannot come *"over the top"*, you cannot have an *"all arms"* swing, and you cannot *"chop down at the golf ball"*.

Reprogramming the Sequence:

Once a 1...3...2...golf swing sequence is "hard wired" into our "swing memory", can it be reprogrammed to fire in sequence? Absolutely; and it won't take very long if you follow this simple drill.

First you have to get a heavy golf club. I'm not a gadget promoter, I don't use gadgets to teach with and I don't see much use for most of them except for a heavy golf club. Swinging a heavy golf club will strengthen your golf muscles, improve your balance by exposing poor balance at any point in the golf swing, train your target hand to be the *Boss* of the golf club, and improve and re-train your swing sequence. Swing your heavy club a few minutes a day in a deliberate attempt to separate your rotations in the

Figure 34
This sequence shows
the 1...3...2...golf swing

Figure 35
This sequence shows the 1...2...3...swing,
notice the club head lag in the middle
picture when the engine turns first

proper sequence. Count out loud the three parts of the golf swing and exaggerate the separations in ¼ speed, and be deliberate in separating the three parts of the swing. This will reprogram the swing sequence so when you get to the golf course, it will happen automatically.

Notes:

10 "C.O.G. and the Driver"

Have Problems Hitting Driver?

Getting the ball off the tee and in play consistently with the driver continues to be a struggle for most players. There are three things working against us when we have the ball on a tee with a driver. Once we understand what happens and how to fix it, we're on our way to long, straight, consistent driver shots. Let's talk about the three problems first, and then the easy fixes using the C.O.G. method.

The problem with the driver is the change in the geometry of the swing due to the placement of the golf ball. We all know we have to place the ball forward in our stance in order to get the ball in the air. Your driver only has about twice as much loft as your putter, so if you hit it off your Center of Gravity the ball will fly very low. The problem then becomes where do you place the ball? There was a study done on the stance and ball position of amateur golfers, and in 10 driver set-ups, no 2 were in the same place. No wonder we have a problem with driver consistency since the geometry of the driver swing and set up are always different. So the first thing we need to do is find a way to set the driver up the same way every time.

The second problem we have is the placement of the club head at the address position. We always place the club head up to the golf ball, which further changes the geometry of the set up making it extremely difficult to manipulate the consistency triangle for solid, straight driver shots.

Figure 36
Showing an "in balance" finish position with feet still in control of the ground and the "Boss hand" in control of the club

The Third problem we have is a visual problem. Since the golf ball is not where it usually is, our eyes will draw our triangle out of position during the golf swing causing the consistency triangle to be way out of shape at the impact position. The good news is, the Center of Gravity triangle set up is exactly the same as it is with your 7 iron, or pitching wedge, it doesn't change with different clubs. Let's break this down and learn the C.O.G. *"can't miss"* driver set up.

Problem 1) Ball Position:

Driver ball position is the first thing we have to solidify in order to be a consistent driver of the golf ball. Getting the ball in the same place every time is difficult because we don't have a solid reference point like we do with our irons (C.O.G., or Shirt button). Setting up the driver ball position to be consistent is easier than you think if you just follow these five steps.

Step 1: Address the ball with your feet together, toes touching, and the ball on your C.O.G. (shirt button).

Step 2: Turn your left toe out a little leaving your heel where it is (do not step out, just turn your toe) to unlock your engine in order to complete your finish position.

Step 3: Take your normal width stance with your right foot. Don't go too wide with your driver stance; just take your normal stance so your engine can do its job properly.

Figure 38	**Figure 39**	**Figure 37**
Feet together, ball on C.O.G.	Turn left toe out	Take stance with right foot

Now your ball is always in the same position, giving you a level of set up consistency your may have never had before.

Problem 2) Placing the head of the Driver:

The second problem we have with driver set up is the placement of the head of the driver in relation

to the golf ball at the address position. After we have our stance and ball position set, almost every golfer places the head of the golf club up next to the ball.

This seemingly insignificant move really plays havoc with your consistency triangle. The first change is that your C.O.G. is now too close to the ball and the bottom of your swing is in the wrong place (too close to the ball). The second problem with placing your club head up to the ball is the direction your shoulders are pointing. Remember the golf club path follows the line of your shoulders and when you place your club head up to the ball, your shoulders are aiming 50+ yards left of your intended target. Here's the easy fix for that.

Step 4: After you have taken your stance, place your driver head back on your C.O.G. (shirt button), which will be 3 to 4 inches behind the golf ball where it should be. Now this spot becomes the bottom of your swing and the club head has a chance to swing up to the ball and sweep it off the tee. Notice how your consistency triangle is in tact and is the same as every other club in your bag and your shoulders are pointing down the target line and not way left as they were before. Now you're ready to make the same 1...2...3...golf swing we learned earlier and maintain your consistency triangle. Next we have to deal with problem # 3.

Problem 3) The Visual Problem:

The visual problem we have with the driver has to do with the ball position and maintaining the consistency triangle during the swing. When you focus your eyes on the golf ball, during dynamic motion your eyes will draw your Center of Gravity toward the ball during the down swing. This is the reaction that allows us to hit a moving baseball or tennis ball. In golf however, we cannot allow our C.O.G. to move toward the ball as this will change the shape of our triangle, causing a change in the geometry of the swing and a miss hit or miss directed shot. If you have ever hit the dreaded "pop up" shot that puts a scar on the top of your new driver, your eyes have drawn your C.O.G. past the point where the golf ball is teed, changing the bottom of your swing dramatically.

The visual problem we have is constantly changing the bottom of our swing, and the amount of the change results in different kinds of miss hits and ball flights. I feel that this is the reason we have so much difficulty with driver consistency. Now we have to solidify the consistency triangle so the bottom of our swing will happen in the same place every time. Here's the solution I use with all my students, and it works every time.

Figure 41
Triangle intact
at address

Figure 43
The "visual problem" pulling
my C.O.G. off center

Figure 42
Using a "Decoy" to hold
my C.O.G. in place

Step 5: Once you have your set up complete with your club head placed back on your C.O.G., place a tee or a marker of some kind in, or on, the ground opposite your C.O.G. (shirt button). This is your "Decoy". The decoy is the key to stabilizing your Center of Gravity Triangle and creating consistency in your tee shots. As with your 5 or 7 iron *(never let your cheek pass the ball)* use the tee or marker and never allow your cheek to pass the decoy. The first few times you use this method on the driving range don't even look at the ball, keep your eye on the decoy and maintain your C.O.G. triangle. You'll be pleasantly surprised at the results you achieve. Once your triangle is used to staying put, you can discard the decoy, if you start to move your triangle again (you will know by the miss hits and erratic ball flight), you can re-instate the decoy for a while longer.

I still use a decoy when I play; if I miss a drive or 2, I will bang the heel of my driver into the ground opposite my C.O.G. Nobody knows what I'm doing and now I have a decoy to stabilize my triangle. Using the decoy will dramatically increase your success off the tee and stabilizing the C.O.G. triangle is the key to consistency. Once you understand why your C.O.G. is moving, and how to maintain it, you will hit the longest and straightest drives of your life.

You now have the knowledge and understanding to complete the simple but powerful 1…2…3…Center of Gravity golf swing. Understanding the Center of Gravity Triangle and how to control it will make you a more consistent striker of the golf ball and eliminate the frustration factor experienced by almost every golfer to play the game. Once you stabilize and understand that the movement of the triangle affects the bottom of your swing, you will quickly become more consistent. This is true for every golf swing you take in every situation, and even more so with the driver because of the set up and the tendency to sway into the ball causing the triangle to get out of shape.

Notes:

11 "Ball Position"

I remember when we were taught 6 or 7 different ball positions depending on what club you were swinging at the time. When you move your ball position, you must also move your C.O.G. triangle to match. This causes you to have a lot of different golf swings to try to make contact with the ball. No wonder, as a group of golfers, we are frustrated since the more compensating movements we have in the golf swing, the more inconsistent we become.

Now that we understand the C.O.G. triangle and how to control it, we need concern ourselves with only one thing. ***Where do I want the bottom of my swing to happen?*** When you decide this, simply place your C.O.G. and club head on that spot and swing your 1...2...3...effortless power swing and control your triangle. The good news is, there is only 1 set up, and 3 ball positions you will need to learn to execute almost every golf shot you make. They are all based on your C.O.G. triangle.

Ball Position 1:

When you have an iron in your hands or a high lofted utility club (Hybrid Club) or even a 9, 11 or 13 wood, you play the ball on your C.O.G. (Shirt Button). These clubs were designed to play at the very bottom of your swing so the club head goes through the ball at a slightly downward angle causing a shallow divot in the ground just ahead of where the ball lies. This is the position where your C.O.G. triangle dissects the golf ball at the bottom.

Ball Position 2:

Ball Position number 2 is for your fairway woods. Fairway woods are designed to be hit on the "Flat" with a sweeping blow in order to launch the ball at the desired trajectory for long distance fairway shots. This type of shot requires you to place your C.O.G. triangle approximately 1" behind the position of the ball so the bottom of your swing happens just before contact, allowing the fairway wood to bottom out and contact the ball on the flat part of the swing. Always remember to place your club head on your C.O.G. (not up to the ball) and fire your *Piston* just the same as your iron shots so you compress the ball and watch it soar. The key to this shot is maintaining your triangle and not allowing your C.O.G. to slide toward the ball during the downswing. If required, place a decoy on your C.O.G. (a tee or a marker of some kind) and do not allow your cheek to pass the decoy. This will hold your triangle in place until you get used to this set up.

Ball Position 3:

Ball Position number 3 is of course the Driver ball position. The Driver is designed to hit the ball on the upswing and therefore the bottom of your swing must happen a few inches behind your ball position. When you follow the driver set up steps described a few pages back in the book, your ball position will always be correct. Your driver usually only has about twice as much loft as your putter so it must be hit on the upswing in order to create the perfect launch conditions for long soaring drives. Golfers who are constantly playing with tee height in order to make solid contact can finally settle into a consistent tee height once they understand how to control their C.O.G. Triangle.

As you can see, ball position is only relevant to where your C.O.G. is located. If you forget about the physical position of the golf ball and simply place your C.O.G. and club head where you want the bottom of your swing to happen, maintain your C.O.G. Triangle, and swing 1...2...3... then consistency and frustration free golf shots will soon follow.

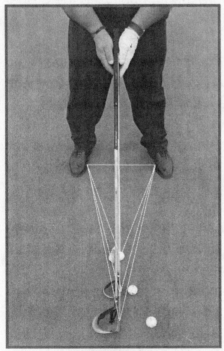

Figure 44
The C.O.G. Triangle is
always the same

Figure 45
The 3 basic ball
positions

Distance from the ball:

One of the great benefits we get from learning to swing the golf club in the C.O.G. 1...2...3...method is that gravity always takes the golf club to the same place at the bottom of your swing. Most players I see stand a little too far away from the golf ball at the address position. I believe this is because most golfers start their swing from the top down; this is the 1...3...2...golf swing we talked about earlier. The 1...3...2...golf swing pushes the club-head to the outside, forcing the player to stand too far away from the ball in order to make contact. Here is the easy method to be sure the golf ball is in the proper place every time.

1) Take your address position ensuring your weight is properly distributed on your feet with pressure on the knuckles of your big toes.

2) Place the club-head into position behind the ball and take your trailing hand off the club *(right for right handed)*.

3) Allow your trail hand to relax and hang naturally from the shoulder and bring it back to the club.

4) Adjust your distance from the ball so your trail hand fits perfectly where it should on the club.

5) This is the proper distance from the golf ball for all your shots...no more guessing.

Figure 46
Reaching for the ball

Figure 47
Crowding the ball, too close

Figure 48
Perfect distance from the ball, C.O.G. Triangle is intact

Notes:

"Golf... The Strategic Battle"

The "game" of golf is really a strategic battle between you and the golf course you're playing. As the golfer, you're trying to get your golf ball into the hole while the golf course is putting obstacles and things in your way in order to make it difficult for you, *and* the golf course has Mother Nature on its side! Wind, rain, heat, bugs, pests, etc. are all there trying to throw your concentration off as you try to negotiate your ball around the course, taunting you into a loss of concentration and a poor shot.

It always surprises me how golfers go to battle with the golf course day after day with no specific plan of attack. A wise General once said *"It's better to have a plan and be wrong, than to never have a plan at all".* Truer words have never been spoken, especially when it comes to the "game" of golf. I see a game of golf as a strategic battle with the golf course. In order to win, or even advance, you must have a plan of attack for the course, and follow that plan. A Touring Professional will have a very detailed plan of attack for the golf course he or she is facing in order to give them the best possible chance of beating the golf course on that day. The Tour Player dissects every hole, every shot, giving them the greatest opportunity to beat that particular hole they're playing by making a birdie or better. Sometimes they win, sometimes they tie (par) and sometimes the golf course wins... as long as the player wins or ties the majority of the 18 battles of the day, they win the war and collect a nice check.

Your battle may not be with par, yours may be with bogey, or double bogey; it really doesn't matter as long as you identify it and create a plan to win. The more battles you win, the lower your handicap gets, and the more challenging the game gets, hence the never ending lure of golf. I know it's not fair to compare our game with that of the Touring Professional, or expect to have as intricate a plan as they do since they have a caddie to help them map out and plan a strategy to attack the hole. They also spend the hours of the day while we're at work practicing specific shots, yardages, and options to help them win as many battles as they can with the golf course.

If we are to start winning more battles, having and implementing a plan is the answer. We all know golfers plateau with their game...they become an 85 shooter, or a 90 shooter and they seem to stay there, never really improving. I truly believe *(and I've seen it a thousand times)* when you have and implement a plan for each hole you can, and will, improve on a steady basis... and then you really can't help winning more battles.

The biggest problem we face is the guesswork that plagues us when we have an uncomfortable distance to carry the ball to the green, especially if there are hazards guarding the green that love to swallow up new white golf balls. Ponds, bunkers, streams, out of bounds, and countless other hazards put there to intimidate us, do just that. The major reason they intimidate us so much is that we are always guessing at the shot we have to hit in order to avoid the hazard and get the ball safely on the putting surface. When we are guessing at what it will take to get the ball safely on the green we create doubt in our minds and in our stroke, inevitably miss hitting our shot, creating another doubt filled shot, or a penalty stroke if we happen to find a hazard.

The majority of the extra shots in our golf games happen from inside 50 yards of the green. This is the area of the golf course where we need to possess, and implement, a game plan. The average golfer in North America (mid handicapper) will hit on average 3 greens in regulation in a round of golf. This means he/she is in this *"scoring zone"* a minimum of 15 times during a round of golf. How many times have you been down in front of the green in 2 shots and then end up taking 4 (or more) shots to get the ball into the hole? THIS is where a plan will bring your game to the next level. The simple math tells us if you implement a plan successfully only 1 out of every 3 times you attempt the shot, you will save a **minimum of 5 shots** off your scorecard. The more confident you become with the plan, the more shots you will shave off your score. On a good ball striking day, I will hit 9 or 10 greens in regulation, and in order for me to shoot even par or under par, my short game and finesse game plans had better be working... and they do! If you are a 95 shooter now, once you implement "The Plan" you will be shooting in the 80's in no time.

Let's get smart and create a plan that WILL change your golf game and lower your scores permanently.

I have formulated, use, and teach such a plan with great success. The following short game plan will encompass the 4 short games in golf, the Chipping game, the Finesse game, the Pitching Game, *the green side bunker shot*, and putting. *(I know that's 5, but I threw in the Green side bunker shot for good measure).* Understanding and putting this plan into action will virtually guarantee lower scores the first time you use it.

Let's have a closer look at *"The Plan"* and how to put it together to take the guesswork out of your short games, start winning more battles and reduce your handicap…guaranteed!

"The Short Game"

C.O.G. and the Short Game

Everything we've talked about so far in the book has to do with consistency and reducing the frustration factor of the long game by understanding why we miss golf shots. While this will certainly save us some strokes in our games, the C.O.G. short game method is designed to create consistency by understanding ball position and learning one simple move that, when put together with the "plan", will save you at least one shot every three holes. This will take you to a new plateau in your golf game. One shot every three holes will turn the 85 shooter into a 79 shooter, and a 95 shooter into an 85 shooter. These are significant improvements and the short game section of this book is designed to do just that, and to do it quickly.

We will learn the easy to execute and easy to understand 1...1...finesse and chipping stroke and the 1...2... pitch shot swing that will simplify your short game and give you more confidence around the green than ever before.

In the Putting section of the C.O.G. short game, we will understand why we miss short putts and three putt so often. We'll talk about the putting set up, stroke and alignment, and the magic move to eliminate three-foot putt anxiety, as well as 2 putting drills guaranteed to improve your putting quickly and easily.

The Four Short Games of Golf:

The first thing we have to do is identify Golf's 4 short games and separate them so we can understand how to break them down and use the C.O.G. method to become good short game players.

The four short games in golf beginning from hole outward are:

1) Putting

2) Chipping

3) Finesse Shots

4) Pitch Shots

We will break these games down and use the C.O.G. short game method to get the ball on the green and in the hole as quickly and efficiently as possible. Lets start just off the green, move back to the pitch shot, and finish with the putting game.

12 "Chipping"

Short Game # 1... Chipping:

Let's start with some simple chipping facts. I believe the chipping stroke is very underestimated by the casual, and in some cases, even low handicap golfers. Chipping, in my opinion is the number two stroke saver in the game behind only putting. I think we should give it a little attention and learn to get the ball close to the hole using all the tools we have available to us.

Let's face it, as a group of weekend or casual golfers we only hit on average 4 – 6 greens in regulation in a round of golf if we're striking the ball well. The very best players in the world average 12 to 14 greens in regulation per round so they have to be able to get it up and down for par or birdie 6 times in a Professional round of golf. We, the golf masses, are expected to do this 12 or more times in a round of golf in order to turn in a half decent score. If we can't consistently get the ball into the hole from the fringe, or from 15 to 25 yards away from the green, we are doomed to play bogey or bogey plus golf for the rest of our lives. As a player, I can remember being frightened every time I missed a green because I knew I'd have to chip and I had no idea where the ball was going to go. When you play this game with fear, you're destined to fail a lot more than you succeed. I was very confused because I'm a good athlete, was doing everything I was told to do and I was not succeeding, not at all. Here's how I was taught to chip the golf ball, see if this rings any bells with you.

1) Play the ball off your back foot.

2) Grip down on the shaft of your golf club.

3) Open your body to the target (turn to the left).

4) Lean a little toward the target, 60% weight on your left foot.

5) Hit the ball with a descending blow, like you're chipping it under a bench using only the big muscles of your back and shoulders.

Sound Familiar? I was taught to chip this way and I am guilty of teaching this method myself as a new Professional making my way in the golf world. I never got any better using this method and I'm sure my clients did not improve much either, so I apologize to those I taught this method to...this is my redemption.

When I developed the C.O.G. method for consistency in the long game, it only made sense to me that it would work in the short game as well, and it does! Let's break this down so it makes sense and works.

Figure 49
The set up I was taught. C.O.G. Triangle is 8" in front of the ball

1) Ball Position: (Remember your C.O.G.?)

The most important factor to making consistent, clean ball contact is understanding ball position. If we follow the advice of the old way (play the ball off your back foot, and lean forward), your C.O.G. (the bottom of your swing) is 8 inches in front of the ball. Now you have to take your right hand and hit down trying to "find" the ball. The problem with this is you cannot control distance, consistency in contact, trajectory, or ball spin. How can you be expected to be consistent if you can't control any of these things? When you use your right hand to hit down on your chip shots you are at the mercy of the "fast twitch" muscles in your hands and forearms to control delicate distances and create clean contact with the golf ball. This is a tall order; in fact, it's hit and miss at best.

We have to be sure of where the bottom of our swing is going to be and make sure the ball is there. As we learned from the full swing, the bottom of your swing will always be on your C.O.G. when your target hand (the one with the glove) is in charge of the club. So let's start there; the ball always goes on your C.O.G., and that way you never have to go looking for it. (More about this later.)

2) The Grip: (Disengaging the Piston)

In the long game portion of the book we learned that we must have 2 rotations in the golf swing in order to make the golf ball fly straight and far. We called the second rotation our *Piston* and learned that it's the compression rotation of the golf swing. This is a very powerful rotation and can be used in the short game by only a very few, highly skilled players.

When you are around the green, in order to begin to control your short game distances, you must disengage your *Piston*. By disengaging your *Piston*, you take away the compression rotation of the swing (you don't need it when you're close) and can start gauging with accuracy the distance of your chip shots. If you've ever hit a chip shot that you thought was good, only to see the ball rocket to the other side of the green into the rough, bunker, or pond, you know what I'm talking about; this was your *Piston* at work.

In order to disengage your *Piston* for the short game, you must rotate your left hand toward the target and grip the club from underneath, placing your thumb on top of the club shaft. Now you can mark the thumb of your glove with your "Finesse Arrow" that will point at the hash mark on your grips. This will act as a reminder to disengage your *Piston* when you get around the green. Be careful not to just turn your

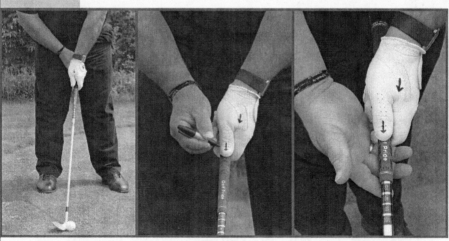

Figure 52	**Figure 51**	**Figure 50**
Disengage your	Mark your "Finess	Grip down so 1 finger
Piston	Arrow"	touches the shaft

thumb on top of the grip as this will *look* disengaged but can still rotate and wreak havoc on your short game. Make sure you completely disengage your *Piston* before setting up to a short game shot.

Grip Down?

In the short game as with the long game, the top 3 fingers of your target hand (the one with the glove) is the *Boss* of the golf club. The pinky, the ring, and the middle finger have to control the club or you get a hitting motion when the right hand gets involved. I like to see my students and players grip down until the index finger of the trail hand is touching the shaft. This is not a magic grip down distance, just a consistent one you can be sure is the same every time. The only reason I can see that we must grip down is to make it easier for our *Boss* fingers to control the golf club for a delicate shot. By gripping down a little, you lighten the club head enough to keep control easily with the *Boss* hand. If you do not grip down a little, the inertia of the club head swinging back may place pressure on the index finger of the trail hand, resulting in a sharp descending blow that will miss the bottom of the swing causing a miss hit chip.

Always Aim Left:

Remember it takes 2 rotations in order to make a golf ball fly straight. If you remove the compression rotation from the golf swing (the *Piston*), you had better aim left of your target because you're going to hit it to the right.

Here's what you do. Take a narrow stance and place the golf ball on your C.O.G.. Disengage your *Piston*, grip down a little and turn **both toes** toward the target at the same time. Now the ball **appears** to be on your back foot, but it is still on your C.O.G. right at the bottom of your swing. Learning this set-up move will ensure solid, consistent contact time after time because the golf ball is where it should be, at the bottom of your swing. Always remember your shoulders must also point left of your target, along

Figure 53
Aiming left in order to get the ball to go at the target with *Piston*: disengaged and cheek not passing the ball

the line of your toes, as this will ensure the ball flies straight to the target. If your shoulders are square to the target, and your *Piston* is disengaged, you will miss to the right.

Don't let your cheek pass the ball:

Once you've set up your short game shot in this manner, it's very hard to make a mistake; the only thing you can do to miss is move your center of gravity during the swing. Since the shot is very short, you need remember only one thing…don't let your cheek pass the ball. If your cheek passes the ball during the stroke, your C.O.G. has moved and so has the bottom of your swing. This will result in a thin shot that will rocket across the green, and we've seen enough of those.

The 1…1…Golf Swing:

As I was saying earlier about how I was taught to chip the golf ball, I was told to only use the large muscles of my back and shoulders to execute the shot. Turn on your television this weekend and see how many players, who feed their families with their golf games, chip in this manner. I can safely say you won't see any of them doing this. The chip shot you see from a Professional is a smooth, rhythmical, motion that always ends up with the engine to the target. They use primarily their bodies to propel the golf ball to the target; I call this the 1…1…swing. Remember the full, powerful golf swing consists of three distinct pieces.

With the short game we take away two of the three pieces in order to gain control of our short distances. The 1...1...swing is an **"All Engine"** swing. Nothing moves unless the Engine moves it. That means there is no "push" away from the ball like the full swing, and there is no *Piston* release through the ball either. There is only Engine back, Engine through. With the Engine back, Engine through golf swing, there is no input from your hands or arms...only the speed of the Engine moving propels the ball to its location. This is how we can predict short game distances.

A Short 7 to 5 motion:

The chipping motion is a very simple 7 o'clock to 5 o'clock motion using only your engine to propel the club head. If the golf ball is sitting at 6 o'clock, simply turn your belt buckle back to the 7 o'clock

Figure 54	Figure 55	Figure 56
Set up with ball on your C.O.G., it only appears to be back in our stance	Shows ball on C.O.G., engine and club head at 7 o'clock position	Engine and club head at 5 o'clock position, ball heading for target

position (with the club following), and back through to the 5 o'clock position on the other side, making sure the club head stays with your belt buckle the whole way. Your engine is a slow twitch muscle that you control, and will rotate at a very consistent rate of speed. This is how you are going to gauge the distances for your chip shots. With your engine in control of your club head speed, you can build a predictable arsenal of shots around the green.

Don't Stall your Engine:

The chipping motion I was taught had no Engine, only the large muscles of my back and shoulders. I suppose this is the only way to propel the ball forward if you don't have an Engine. Now that you do have an Engine, don't stall it. If you stall your Engine, you have no power to the club head and have to resort to a "hit" with your hands and arms. We know now that this produces un-predictable results and costs us big time on the scorecard. Always keep your Engine moving toward the target as this will ensure predictable distances with your chipping clubs.

Have a favorite chipping club?

Are you the type of player that chips with the same club all the time? Most amateurs and weekend players do just this. I think by doing this you are complicating the process of getting the balls close as opposed to making it easier. When you use one club to chip with, you have to make up dozens of swings in order to achieve the distance and roll out

Figure 57
Using the basic 7 - 5 chipping move and most of your clubs will quickly build a strong chipping game

numbers you need to get the ball close. If you always use your Pitching Wedge for instance, a 6 yard chip swing would look a lot different than a 15 yard chip swing. Therefore, you are always guessing at how hard to "hit" the ball to get it to go the desired distance. Wouldn't it be easier to have one basic move (7 - 5, *Engine, Engine*) and use different tools to get the desired distance? You bet it is.

Once you've perfected your 1…1…chipping swing using the 7 - 5 motion, go to your local golf course and practice this for a little while. Start with the most lofted club in your bag, hit 10 chip shots using the 7 - 5 motion and see how far they go. Now do the same with your Pitching Wedge, 9-iron, 8-iron and so on.

You will soon see how easy it is to create the desired chipping distance using different tools and the same swing.

Have a Plan:

Having a plan when you chip the golf ball will not only increase your chances of success, but will also increase your confidence. Any sports psychologist will tell you that increased confidence will result in better execution of the golf shot, and better execution results in increased confidence and so on. When you know (and are confident with) the 7 - 5 chipping distances of all your clubs…(including your rescue clubs, and high lofted woods), you have taken the guesswork out of your short game and built in shot saving confidence.

I am going to include some carry and roll ratios worked out on a medium speed, flat green. This will help you understand how different clubs can help you score better around the green.

Carry and Roll Ratios:

These carry and roll ratios were worked out on a medium speed, flat green, and will give you a starting point to build a short game arsenal that will lower your scores today.

Sand Wedge:
Carry 3 yards –
Roll out 1 Yard,
total = 4 yards

Pitching Wedge:
Carry 1 yard –
Roll out 2 yards,
total = 3 yards

9-Iron:
Carry 1 yard –
Roll out 3 yards,
total = 4 yards

8-Iron:
Carry 1 yard –
Roll out 4 yards,
total = 5 yards

7-Iron:
Carry 1 yard –
Roll out 5 yards,
total = 6 yards

Now you can start to build a game plan around the green that will enable you to get the ball close by using 1 basic move (Engine, Engine…7 - 5) by seeing the different carry and roll out ratios of each club in your bag. Take out the guesswork by having a plan, and you will chip it close the majority of the time, and perhaps even chip some in.

Figure 58
Using a chipping target to see my landing zone

This brings me to the next subject, your target.

Find your Target:

Knowing what your target is, and identifying it, is critical to becoming a good chipper of the golf ball.

The first thing you must understand is that the hole is not your target in a chip shot. Your target is a spot on the green (preferably a flat spot) where you want to land the ball so it can roll like a putt to the hole. Once you know your 7 - 5 yardages with your clubs, you can predict your landing area, and then from that spot you can read the chip like a putt so you can predict break and slope. This is important for getting the ball close (and even holing out a few chip shots), understanding where the ball is going to land, and how the green will react from the spot to the hole.

Now you're putting the puzzle together. A wise General once said; *"It is always better to have and execute a plan and be wrong, than never to have had a plan at all."* Having a plan when chipping is a sure fire way to bring your score down the next time you play.

A Tip...

If you can't remember the distances of your 7 - 5 chip shots with all your clubs, wrap a piece of masking tape around the top of the shaft, right under the grip, and write the distance on it. It's perfectly legal and will give you all the confidence you need to pull the shot off, which brings me to our next short game, the Finesse Shot.

Notes:

13 "The Finesse Game"

Short Game # 2... The Finesse Shot:

The "Finesse Game" is a very important part of the short game arsenal you need in order to build your confidence around the green and bring your game to a new plateau. The finesse game is what I call the awkward, in between distances that we never get a chance to practice. The 15-yard, 25-yard, 35-yard in the air shot we all need and are always guessing at are the delicate shots around the green that often cost us many strokes on the scorecard.

The Webster's Dictionary defines "Finesse" as (*a subtly skillful handling of a situation*). I remember very clearly when I started to take this sport seriously, the swings I made when I found myself in these awkward, short distances, were neither subtle, nor skillful. I was always guessing at how hard to hit the ball, what club to use, and so on. This creates an air of doubt every time you face the shot, and you face this shot more often than you think.

I can predict with some confidence, that you will face a finesse shot on average 9+ times per round, sometimes more. These shots almost always present themselves in a "pressure situation" where you have to carry a pond, creek, bunkers, or other form of hazard and somehow get the ball to stop on the green without rolling off the other side. You can't hit it too hard, but you can't hit it too soft or you'll be in the hazard, so what do you do? These are the times you need a plan, you need to know what a 25 yard in the air shot is...you need a finesse shot.

What is a Finesse shot?

A finesse shot is a high, lofted shot that travels a pre-determined distance in the air. Pre-determined being the optimal word here. These are very reliable, very repeatable shots that, when used with confidence, will increase your success around the greens dramatically. Now that you know how to execute with confidence the *1...1... (Engine... Engine)* golf swing, you have the move to create these reliable "Finesse Shot" distances whenever you need them.

Let's set it up:

I've hit my ball short of the green in 2 and I have to carry a small pond to a front pin position. I have a good lie, and its 25 yards to the fringe of the green where I need to land the ball in order to have a serious shot at making par on this hole. My playing partner is on the green in 2 with 30 feet and two puts for Par, so I need to make this shot.

Ever found yourself in a situation like that? Almost every time you play? This is the scenario for any pressure shot around the green when you don't really know what to do. Those short yardage shots and awkward distances are things we just don't have time to practice because, as you know, life gets in the way of golf, even for a teaching Pro like me. Luckily, there is a way to learn this and build an arsenal of these shots you can count on without spending countless hours at the practice range.

The 1…1… Finesse Shot:

We know now how effective the 1…1… golf swing is in the chipping game. The all *Engine* swing that takes out the *Push*, and the *Piston* of the full golf swing will reproduce reliable distances with different tools. The good news is, the Finesse shot is exactly the same move as the 1…1…chip shot but with different clock positions and a hands high finish. Here's how you set it up.

1) Grip down on your club (makes it easier to control the club head).

2) Disengage your *Piston* (take out the compression rotation of the swing).

3) Place the ball between your toes on your C.O.G. (where you want the bottom of your swing to happen).

4) Aim Left by turning both toes toward the target (ball appears to be on your back foot and is still on your C.O.G.).

5) Use your "*Engine*" *(1…1…golf swing)* to propel the ball to the target. (now you can control your short game yardages).

This is exactly the same set up as the chip shot, but here's what makes it a "Finesse shot".

Work Your Clock & Finish High:

Figure 59
The difference between a finesse shot and a chip shot...finish high for a high, soft shot

Working your clock simply means hitting 3 different positions on your back swing, which will produce 3 distinct, lofted, distances that will not roll away from you when they land, and that you can count on time and again. The distance the ball travels is dependant on the position of your backswing and the speed of your *Engine*. This is an *Engine back, Engine through* swing using the 7, 9, and 11 o'clock positions on our clock. This swing always finishes with the *Engine* facing the target, hands high, and club head straight up, (12 o'clock) looking past your shaft. This finish position will send the ball high so it lands softly on the green.

The Clock:

The three positions on the clock are: 7 o'clock (you're familiar with that position in the chip shot); 9 o'clock - which is the position of your *Engine* at the top of your swing with the golf club in (the "L" position); and the 11 o'clock - which is as far as your *Engine* will turn away comfortably with your hands following. This last position may be 10 or

Figure 60: 7 o'clock   9 o'clock   11 o'clock   Finish HIgh

10:30 for some depending on your range of motion, but it doesn't matter, they will all produce a specific distance in the air when executed with confidence.

Learn the 9 o'clock distance first - it's the easiest to execute because it's the "L" to "L" position, the same on both sides. Go to the driving range or the back yard armed with a few balls, a sand wedge, and a towel. Practice your finesse swing from 9 o'clock to the full finish position using only your *Engine* as a power source. After a few shots you will begin to see a pattern develop. Step off the average distance and place your towel on the ground. Go back to your tee and see how close you can come to your towel with 10 shots. In no time you will have a reliable, repeatable distance with your 9 o'clock finesse shot with your sand wedge. Write it down.

When you are comfortable with this shot, repeat the process with the 7 o'clock, and the 11 o'clock positions making sure to use only your *Engine* as a power source and finishing high, looking past your club shaft. Now you have three finesse distances you can count on with your sand wedge.

Repeat this process with every wedge in your bag and you will have 9-12 short distances you can count on when you need them.

Own these Distances:

It's important that you test these distances on the practice area so you can become confident with, and own, these distances. Being confident in your *Engine's* ability to produce consistent distances, and knowing your clock yardages with each wedge in your bag will give you so much confidence around the green by eliminating the guesswork associated with these types of shots. The more confident you are, the better you execute shots - it's a vicious cycle...in a good way.

Have your Plan Ready:

As with the chipping game, having a plan and executing it with confidence is the key to lowering

Figure 61
Finesse yardages marked on all my wedges

Figure 62
When faced with finesse yardage, always remember to disengage your *Piston* and point your "finesse arrow" to the center mark on your grip

your scores so why not have a plan. **Write your finesse distances on all your wedges**, the same as we did for chipping.

Now when you're faced with the 25 yard over water to a short pin shot, just pull out the wedge that has a 25 written on it and hit your shot. The good news is, I don't care if you hit it 23 yards or 27 yards, you're still going to be close. This plan will allow you to free up your mind and your swing since there's no guesswork - it's written right there on the shaft of your wedge, just trust it and make the shot. Even if you're off by a few yards…who cares, you're on the green and putting for par.

Having these shots in your bag and executing them with confidence will change your golf game quickly, and dramatically. This is a very versatile shot that can be used in many situations around the green.

Where can you apply the Finesse Shot?

There are lots of situations around the green where you can apply this finesse type of shot, let's look at a few.

1) **Over a Hazard close to the green**:
   This is the obvious scenario we already went over earlier, nice to have a shot for this situation.

2) **Over a Steep embankment, guarding the green**:
I'm sure you've been in this situation before; you're at the bottom of a hill, looking up at the green. If you chip the ball up the hill, or bump an iron into the hill hoping to bounce the ball up on the green somewhere, the risk is that they might not jump up, and may roll back down the hill at your feet, or you may bump the ball too far across the green leaving another chip shot coming back. The finesse shot will loft the ball up on the green and it will stay put, allowing you a putt to save par.

3) **Off the top of a hill, looking down at the green:**
If you find yourself from time to time looking down at the green from on top of a hill, or from a high mound surrounding the green,

you may need a shot for this predicament. If you bump your 7-iron or wedge down the hill you run the risk of the ball getting caught in the long grass, leaving you another chipping situation. Or if you try to bump your 7-iron onto the putting surface, it may run off the back of the green into more trouble. Using the finesse shot in this situation will ensure the ball lands on the green and stays there, giving you an opportunity to make a putt.

14 "Greenside Bunkers & Pitch Shots"

Greenside Bunker:

Greenside bunker? If you're the player who has problems with the greenside bunker shot, here's your solution. **A greenside bunker shot is nothing more than a finesse shot with a ball position adjustment.**

The greenside bunker shot is a very easy shot to execute if you use the exact same set up as the finesse shot, and use your *Engine* to propel the sand and ball onto the green. The only change is ball position. One of the major problems I see with any bunker shot is poor ball position. Once you understand the C.O.G. method of ball position and where the bottom of your swing is, the bunker set up is easy and repeatable.

Figure 63
Take your stance with the ball opposite your left toe, leaving your C.O.G. a couple of inches behind the ball

We understand our swing will bottom out on our Center of Gravity so we have to make sure our C.O.G. is 2 or 3 inches behind the ball, where we want the club to enter the sand. To achieve the perfect ball position every time, simply adopt this small change. Take a narrow stance and instead of placing the ball on your C.O.G., place the ball opposite your left toe. Now turn both toes at the same time toward your target and the ball will be in the proper spot at the bottom of your swing, every time. Disengage your *Piston* and grip the club firmly with your *Boss* fingers.

Now the shot is a simple, *Engine* back, *Engine* through Finesse swing with your *Engine* finishing facing the target and hands high, looking past your club shaft.

When you use this bunker set up and swing, you can start to gauge the distance of your bunker shots the same as you did with your Finesse yardages by working your clock in the bunker.

Never Stall your Engine:

A stalled *Engine* is the number one cause of poor bunker shots and poor short game shots in general. Greenside bunker shots that are left in the sand are almost always due to a stalled *Engine*. If you stall your *Engine* in the bunker and rely on your arms and hands to get the ball out, there is often not enough momentum to push the sand from the bunker and carry the ball out, many times resulting in another bunker shot,

Figure 64
Turn "both" toes toward the target at the same time, leaving your C.O.G. behind the ball

Figure 65
A stalled engine in the bunker almost always leads to another bunker shot

or a very short shot that doesn't make it to the putting surface. Using your *Engine* to splash the sand out of the bunker will produce the momentum required to get the job done easily, time after time.

When facing any short game shot, especially a greenside bunker shot, your ultimate goal should be to have your *Engine* get its job done. You will produce consistent shots and reduce dramatically the "flub" shots that cost us so many strokes around the greens, and in the bunkers.

Figure 66 Using your engine to power the ball out of the bunker will produce reliable results

Short Game # 3...The Pitch Shot:

I put the pitch shot in a short game section of its own because we have to make 2 small adjustments in order to distinguish it from the Finesse shot. A pitch shot is basically any shot that is outside your longest Finesse shot yardage and inside your full swing wedge distances. For example, if your full swing sand wedge distance is 80 yards, and your longest Finesse sand wedge distance is 40 yards, in between 40 yards and 80 yards you require another shot...this is the pitch shot. Remember your full swing yardage requires the 1...2...3...full swing sequence, and your Finesse shot, and chip shot require the short shot producing the 1...1...Finesse golf swing. The pitch shot, or in-between shot, calls for the 1...2...swing.

The 1...2...Golf Swing:

The 1...2...golf swing is exactly the same as the 1...1...Finesse golf swing with one difference.

The 1...2...3...full swing requires a separation between the three pieces of the golf swing in order to create maximum power and ball speed.

The 1...1...Finesse golf swing takes away the *Push*, and the *Piston*, leaving only *Engine*, *Engine* to get the job done creating consistent, reliable short shots.

The 1...2...Pitch shot golf swing uses the same *Engine* back, *Engine* through move as the Finesse swing but we engage and release the *Piston* through the hitting area.

By engaging and adding the *Piston* to the 1...1...Finesse golf swing, we can fill in those yardages between the Finesse shot and the full swing shot. Adding the *Piston* to these Finesse shots we've already learned will give you even more yardages you can count on, and the difference is very dramatic.

For instance, a 9 o'clock Finesse shot with my 56 degree sand wedge will produce a 25-yard in the air shot time after time; I know that and have it written on the club shaft. When I make the same move and add the *Piston* the shot becomes 50 yards in the air. That's a 25-yard difference, just by adding the *Piston* to the shot. The pace of the *Engine* back, and *Engine* through are the same but we engage our *Piston* by pointing our power arrow down the center of the grip. Allow your *Piston* to naturally rotate at the bottom of your swing and you will have a pitch shot you can count on with every wedge in your bag.

Now that you have this move, try it with your 9, 8, and 7 irons and see what they do, you might be surprised at the shots you have that you never knew you had.

Don't forget to square your stance:

Always remember with your short game shots, when you *disengage* your *Piston* you *must aim to the left* because you have taken away the second rotation of the golf swing. However, in the pitch shot you have put the *Piston* back in the shot, so you *must square yourself* to the target in order to get the ball to go where you want.

Notes:

15 "C.O.G. and Putting"

Short Game # 4, Putting:

"Putting…a game within a game…might justly be said to be the most important part of Golf"
- Bobby Jones

I've left the putting game to the last not because it's the least important of the short games - it's quite the opposite. The putting game is the most important of the 4 short games in golf because it comprises almost half *(and sometimes more than half)* of all the strokes we take in a round of golf.

The fastest way to reduce your score in golf is to take fewer putts per hole. This has been an accepted truth in golf instruction for as long as I can remember, and I can't disagree with it. Building a solid, confidant, putting game will certainly take your golf game to the next level. If you already have a good putting game, think for a minute what your score would be if you were a poor putter.

I think in order to create a good putting game you can rely on you have to understand the way we think when it comes to our ultimate target, the hole. In the game of golf, the definition of "par" on a hole allows an expert golfer 2 shots on every green to complete the hole in the allotted number of strokes. That's 36 putts per round to shoot an even par score if you hit every green in regulation.

We've already established that the average golfer doesn't hit many greens in regulation, so let's say we had a great ball-striking day and we hit 9 greens in regulation. If we took our regulated 36 putts to complete the round, we would shoot 81. Not bad, but if we converted 6 of the missed greens into 1 putt greens we would shoot 75, big difference. So the question is, how do we convert 1/3 of the greens we miss into 1-putt greens? If we take 1 putt on 1/3 of the greens in a round of golf, we lower our score by 6 shots.

That's the simple math, and it should put into perspective the task we have at hand. When broken down, the job doesn't seem so daunting. Taking 1 less putt, every 3 holes is an achievable goal for everybody who plays this game. First, let's think about our target.

We have been taught, either through Professional instruction or personal experience, to be very cautious and careful when putting. I can remember being taught to putt to an imaginary 3-foot circle around the hole when I was 15-20 feet away. I think this style of putting breeds a tentative putting stroke that doesn't flow like the great putters you see on any Tour. This is the very reason we leave mid range and short range putts short of the hole, because we're scared of the 3 foot putt coming back if we miss.

A very smart golf coach once said, *"If you're not trying to hole every putt, you're going to get beaten by someone who is."*. Let's face it, most Tour Events boil down to a putting contest, they all hit it great, they can all chip it close, but it's the putter that makes the difference between 1st and 10th place on the leader board. If a Tour player adopted the attitude we have in the putting game, he or she wouldn't be a tour player for long.

So the first thing we have to do is change our attitude about putting. How do we do this? By building a confident putting set up and putting stroke.

The Set-Up:

The putting set up is very important in a few aspects; the most important is that you are comfortable. I find a lot of golfers are trying to force themselves into a position they see a player do on TV or that their teaching Professional wants to see

Figure 67 using a CD to make sure eyes are over the ball

and they are not comfortable standing over the ball. If you're not comfortable standing over a putt, you will tend to freeze over the ball, questioning yourself on line, speed, etc., which is disastrous. I don't care if you stand with your feet together, apart, or on 1 foot, as long as you are in a comfortable position to execute the stroke. Being comfortable is the first and most important part of a confident putting stroke.

The only "rule" I have is that I like to see your eyes directly over the ball at address. This gives you a "down the line" perspective of the putt and allows you to see the line better.

So how do you achieve the level of comfort needed in order to have a free flowing putting stroke?

Feel Strong at Address:

As with all full swings, you must feel like an athlete when you address your putts. Feeling strong at

Figure 68
Feel
"Strong" in
your putting
stance

address will not only give you the secure feeling of being in balance, but will also stabilize your C.O.G. triangle which, as we will see, is very important to getting the ball started on the line we pick.

Press the knuckles of your big toes into the ground and create your anchors for your triangle. This will keep you from falling away to your heels and pushing the putt off line or altering the C.O.G. triangle causing a miss directed putt. Grip the putter handle lightly and allow the top 3 (*Boss*) fingers of your target hand to be in control. Disengage your *Piston* the same as you would for a chip shot and point your Finesse arrow straight down the shaft. This will prevent your *Piston* from getting involved in the putting stroke, which will create havoc with your distance control if it rotates at the bottom.

Ball Position:

Ball position in the putting set up may be the most important aspect of creating a repeatable, reliable, putting stroke. Some golfers like to have the ball position forward in their stance a little so they can hit up at the ball causing it (they believe) to leave the putter with over spin, and some like to play the ball a little back in their stance to give the ball a descending blow (I believe these are the players with no follow through in their putting strokes).

The truth of the matter is, putters are designed with approximately 4 degrees of loft on the blade. The reason for this is so the putter can lift the ball out of the depression it has created on the putting surface (due to the weight of the ball), and get it on top of the grass and rolling toward the hole quickly, without skipping or sliding.

As far as I can see, the only way the putter can do its job properly is if the golf ball is at the very bottom of the swing arc, on your C.O.G. If the bottom of the swing happens at the bottom center of the golf ball, the putter will do its job and you can begin

Figure 69
The C.O.G. Triangle also applies to your putting set up

to create not only directional stability, but also speed control with your putter. Miss hit putts are the number 1 cause for poor speed on all distance putts. If you do not make contact with the ball on the center of percussion of the putter it's the same as miss-hitting an iron shot thin, or on the toe or heel, you just don't get the same distance or direction results.

By understanding ball position and ensuring the same contact point time and again, you can begin to realize how to control your distances and putt with confidence. Place the ball on your C.O.G., making sure the bottom of your swing will happen at the bottom of the golf ball, lifting it out of the depression and rolling it toward the target.

Equipment:

Figure 70
This off the rack putter does not fit my build or stance

One of the most neglected pieces of golf equipment has to be the putter. This is the most used club we have in our bags and yet we abuse it on a daily basis. We blame the putter for missed putts and slam it against our foot, or back into the bag. We toss it, threaten it with bodily harm, or replacement, when all it's guilty of is doing exactly what we told it to do. Additionally, if the putter is not the right one for your stance or stroke, whose fault is that?

Every time I have a putting clinic or a private lesson I ask the same question, *"How many people here today have their putter custom fit to their stance and stroke?"*. None? One? Certainly never more than three in a group of fifty plus participants. A brand name putter can cost anywhere from $100.00 to $500.00 and up depending on the material and research that went into developing it.

Putters today are very well balanced, thoughtfully designed technology that will help you get the ball in the hole faster *IF* they fit you properly. A $500.00 putter that doesn't fit you properly isn't worth $5.00 because all the technology built into it is not working for you. How can you expect to be comfortable over a putt if the putter is dictating your stance and ball position? And if you are comfortable in your stance, the putter's angles are all off and working against you.

The standard men's length putter is 35" long. Golfers buy a putter off the rack because they like the looks, or the alignment technology it has, or their favorite Pro is using it on TV and you don't think about the implications a poor fit may have to you.

For example, if the putter is too long for you, the toe of the putter may be off the ground at the address position, or if it's too short, the heel may be off the ground. Remember the 4 degrees of loft? If the toe or heel is off the ground at address, the ball will start off line left or right on every stroke. Now you have to either aim a little left or a little right to compensate... but how much? Or if you set the putter up perfectly flat and on line, you're out of your comfortable set up position and forcing a stroke.

Figure 71 My custom putter beside an off the rack putter

These are the things we never think about when purchasing a putter. I always tell my clients, a $200.00 putter that fits you properly costs the same as a $200.00 putter that doesn't fit you. Custom fitting is a service every Pro-Shop should provide, and if they don't, find another Pro-Shop. Let's face it, golf equipment today is an investment and it can, and should, be personalized to you. If you are an E-Bay equipment buyer, remember all bodies are not created equal and you may be getting a great deal on equipment that is not right for you. Custom fitting takes away the poor equipment factor and allows you to think about missed shots as just that...missed, and not equipment issues, so you can focus on making the putt.

I'm a regular height guy, about 5 foot 9" and my putter is 32" long and the shaft is bent 8 degrees flat. This is the position I am comfortable in where the putter blade sits flat of the green and my eyes are directly over the ball. You cannot go into a Pro-Shop anywhere and buy a putter with this combination, however, it took me 10 minutes to adjust the putter to fit me perfectly and your Pro can do the same for you at no charge when you buy a new putter. If you don't want or need to buy a new putter, simply take yours to a certified club maker in your area and have your existing putter fit to you. It may cost you a few dollars but the results and peace of mind will be worth it.

Establish your Rhythm and maintain your Triangle:

Establishing a putting rhythm and maintaining your C.O.G. triangle will turn you into a consistent putter of the golf ball more quickly than any putting drill. Maintaining the C.O.G. triangle is probably the easiest thing to do in theory, but becomes difficult as we get anxious and want to see where the ball is going.

Now that you have taken your putting stance and feel "strong" at address by having your anchors firmly in charge of the ground, all you have to do in order to solidify your C.O.G. triangle is not allow your cheek to pass the ball. If your cheek does not pass the ball until after impact and separation, your triangle will have stayed intact and the ball will start on your intended line. If your cheek passes the ball before impact, your triangle is out of shape and the putters' path has changed, causing a change in initial direction. A good rule of thumb is to never let your cheek pass the bottom of the triangle until the ball is outside of your peripheral vision.

Maintaining your C.O.G. triangle is the key to consistent putter path and gaining trust in your putting stroke. If you watch every player, on any tour you choose, they all have something in common, they maintain the consistency triangle until long after the ball is gone. Some even hold it until the ball stops rolling, just to be sure of no movement; it is imperative that you begin this ritual as well if you hope to become a confident, consistent, putter of the golf ball.

Establishing your putting rhythm is how you create consistency in execution of the putting stroke and create the basis for distance control. You can establish your rhythm easily with a metronome and a few golf balls at your local putting green. Start with a 2-foot putt and set your metronome at 60 beats per minute. Stroke the putts in time with the metronome and see if it feels too slow, too fast, or just right for you. Adjust the beat by 1 or 2 either up or down until you find the perfect "pace" for you. Mine is 66 beats per minute, yours may be slower or faster, depending on your personal body rhythm. Once you discover your rhythm, practice every distance putt using this beat. Always use the same rhythm no matter if you have a 2-foot putt or a 40-foot putt. Establishing and using your personal putting rhythm will help take the guesswork and tentativeness out of your putting stroke, allowing your stroke to flow freely, and roll the ball positively toward the target.

Use your stance as a guide for Distance Control:

Once you have your rhythm established using the metronome, you can gauge the speed of any greens you may be playing away from your home course by taking 3 or 4 minutes to gauge the green speed by using your normal stance.

Playing golf all over the world on a weekly basis we sometimes visit 3 or 4 different golf courses per week and they all have different greens. Some are fast, some are slow, some are Bermuda grass, some are bent grass, and some are a combination of grasses and in differing states of condition. The point is, it sometimes takes 4 or 5 holes before you start to catch on to the speed and grain of the greens. By that time, you may have 3 putted or missed some make-able putts simply because you're not sure of the speed. Every time I visit one of these courses, I take a few minutes to get a feel for the greens and take away the guesswork for the first few holes.

On the practice green, I pick a relatively flat part and stroke putts not to a target, but just to gauge distance. Using my personal putting tempo, I use my natural stance and stroke putts using the putting length (*back toe/front toe*). I will roll 3 to 4 putts using this stroke length and my putting rhythm and make

Figure 72
With shoulders square to the line, the putt rolls straight to the cup

a note of how far they roll. If for example, the (*back toe/front toe*) stroke rolls the ball 12 feet on average, when I get to the first green, I will know what 12 feet is and use this knowledge to get the ball close until I get the feel of the greens. This simple method will give you the confidence to roll the ball freely in the first few holes so you don't get behind early.

The Important Aiming Lines:

This is the time during my clinics that I start to talk about the dreaded 3-foot putt. This is the distance no one wants to have left over and you look longingly at your playing partner silently begging for a "gimmie".

The truth is, we miss way too many of these putts so we like to declare them "gimmies" and get on with

Figure 73
Shoulders visibly open at address will lead to poor
flow lines and lots of missed short putts

it. Problem is, sometimes we have to make them. Local Tournaments, Club Championships, $2.00 Nassau's, or a .25 cent bet with your weekly playing partner are all forms of "pressure situations" where you must sink the 3-foot putt, and no one is giving it to you. If you're not used to making these putts, they can haunt you even before you have one. However, if you understand the reason we miss so many, perhaps they'll be less scary and become almost automatic, like you see on any Pro Tour.

The problem I see with 3-foot putts is the set up and the importance of the shoulder lines. Always remember...the putter, as with any golf swing with any club, will follow the line of your shoulders. As I stated earlier, I don't care if you stand with one foot in front of the other, narrow, wide, or on one foot, the putter will follow the line of your shoulders through the stroke, not the lines of your feet or knees.

If we were built perfectly for this game, we would hold the golf club with one hand over the other, leaving our arms the same length and our shoulder lines pointing straight down the target line. However, we do not hold the golf club in this manner. We always put our right hand down below our left to take the proper grip on our golf club. When we do this, the act of having one hand below the other pushes our right shoulder out in front of our left.

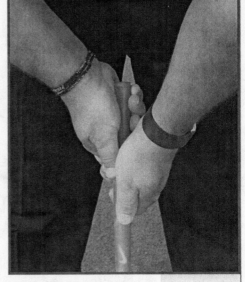

Now if you look closely, from 3 feet, you are actually aiming left of the hole. If you put a good, relaxed putting stroke on the ball, you will miss on the left edge of the hole almost every time. Now you may start to compensate by manipulating your hands through the bottom of the swing to get the ball back on line. When this happens, you have no idea where the ball is going to go from 3 feet. If you remember to square your shoulders up to the intended line of putt and maintain your C.O.G. triangle by controlling your feet and not allowing your cheek to pass the ball, you will have a hard time missing from the 3-foot distance.

This minor adjustment, and understanding of what is happening to your triangle during your putting stroke, will change forever your outlook on those 3-foot knee knockers.

Try Left Hand Low:

If you have trouble pulling your right shoulder back square when putting, try placing your left hand low. Some people call this cross-handed, but it isn't really, it's just left hand below the right. When you set up your grip this way, your shoulders are very square to the line of putt. Personally, I have trouble controlling distance putts like this but it is very good from in close. I prefer to square my shoulders up at address, but if this grip method works for you, use it and start making more putts.

The Trouble with Putting:

There are so many external factors working against us when we putt and the plain truth is that all good putts don't go in. We could do everything right, and stroke the putt perfectly and it might miss because of an external factor beyond our control. Let's have a look at a few things that help us to miss.

1) Architects:

These people take great pride in creating optical illusions and subtle nuances in putting surfaces that goad us into improper alignment, or to strike a putt too softly because it appears to be an uphill putt. I'm sure you have local knowledge of the idiosyncrasies of the greens at your home course, but you only came to know them over time and a number of missed putts, even when someone told you it broke up the hill. The Professionals you watch on TV have an intricate knowledge of the greens they play on, and their caddies have detailed notes on the drainage tendencies and optical illusions built into the putting surfaces, and still they get fooled from time to time. The next time you miss a putt because it went the "wrong way", smile, acknowledge the architect who designed the green, and remember for the next time you have the same putt.

2) Imperfect Putting Surfaces:

As a culture of golfers, I have to say that we are a bit "spoiled" when it comes to putting surfaces. The most complaints I ever hear about a golf course is the condition of the putting surfaces. We all want to play on the greens we see on TV during the Open Championships or the Masters or any PGA Tour Event for that matter. The one thing we don't understand is that these golf courses are closed to play for weeks, sometimes months, before the tournament to prepare the Greens and Fairways for the best players in the world and the TV audience. Your local golf course or the resort course you're playing probably sees 150 to 200 players per day in a lot of cases. That's a lot of footprints, unfixed pitch marks, scrape marks, and trampled down grass in the run of a day to come between your perfectly struck putt, and the hole.

While this may not be as much of a factor on the PGA Tour, it is an every day reality of club and local golf. Unless you belong to a Private club with few members and a low annual round count, you know what I'm talking about. This is a fact of life for the vast majority of golf clubs in North America and we have to stop blaming the superintendents and greens crew for less than perfect conditions. With the growth of the game, sometimes there are just too many players and not enough hours in the day for the greens to remain perfect, or near perfect, day in and day out.

The good news is, they are the same for everyone on that given day. As a very smart colleague of mine pointed out to me one day when I was complaining about the condition of the greens we played in a local Professional Tournament, *"Some players complain, Some players adjust"*. When the winning score came in well below par, it blew my *"poor greens"* excuse right out of the water. That was the last time I complained about the condition of a golf course, in fact, one of the first rules of golf is *"Play the course as you find it"*.

3) **We're always Guessing:**

I say this about putting because golf is the only sport I can think of where you're not looking at the target you're trying to hit. Baseball, football, darts, hockey, bowling, all these sports require you to look at the target you want to hit while you're delivering the ball, dart, or puck to the desired target. Your eyes gather all the information your brain needs in order to get the object to the target and not come up short or send it too far.

Figure 74
Keeping your eyes on your target while attempting long puts will improve your distance control dramatically

Imagine how difficult the game of Darts would be if you looked at the dartboard, picked your target, and then shut your eyes for 4 or 5 seconds before you let the dart fly. I wouldn't want to be anywhere between you and the dart board because your throw would be a total guess. At this pace, a game of darts would take days to play. Or imagine a baseball pitcher staring down the target of his catcher's glove, and then closing his eyes, winding up, and trying to "imagine" where the glove is and deliver a 95-mile per hour fastball in the strike zone. I wouldn't want to be the batter in that scenario.

When we golf however, every time the hole or target is outside our peripheral vision, we're guessing at where it is because we're staring at the golf ball. The problem is, the brain will only hold a distance image for a short while before it starts to think about other things; *"I always miss from this distance", "I can't believe I keep leaving myself these impossible putts" , "I'm going to have to pay again this week", "We need a new superintendent, theses greens are terrible"*, and so on.

By now you've totally forgotten where the hole is and you make a tentative attempt to get the ball where you think you remember the hole is. This is a problem for players who stand over the ball for too long. The last thing you see must be your target, and then you must get the ball rolling toward the target quickly. We'll talk about a drill later on to get you target orientated on the putting greens.

Figure 75
Remembering the last 4 footer I made before I pull the trigger

4) **Your Memory:**

A golfer's worst enemy is their memory and the internalized image of themselves on the golf course. If I talked to you the way you talk to yourself on the golf course, you wouldn't like me very much, let alone buy my book. Golfers berate themselves ruthlessly on the golf course, which firmly implants strong doubt that they can handle any situation they find themselves in.

Calling yourself names and berating your abilities out loud in front of an audience is not the way to gain confidence in your own abilities. Mark Twain once observed *"The inability to forget is infinitely more devastating than the inability to remember"*.

The best players ever to play the game have a very selective memory when it comes to pulling off any golf shot facing them. When faced with a shot of any length or difficulty, they choose to forget all the bad shots and remember the very best shot they ever hit in that situation and go with that feeling and state of mind. The weekend golfer has a much different mindset when playing difficult shots of any kind because of the memory they choose when they stand over the shot.

I know you can remember a day when you rolled in everything you looked at on the green, and I also know you remember the day you couldn't make anything. If you stand over your putt and all you can think about is a negative image of how many you missed recently, you're not in the right frame of mind to let your putting stroke flow freely.

On the other hand, if you remember all the putts you've made from that distance, your mindset is now right to stroke a putt with confidence. If you believe you've done everything right and the ball does not go in, shrug it off and believe the golf course owes you one. If you've obviously made a mistake, just make a mental note of it and try not to let it happen again. Positive affirmation and a positive thought process will go very far in the way you play the game and how you feel about yourself when the game is over.

Putting Drills:

When you don't play this game for a living, life gets in the way of your golf time, let alone your practice time. Casual golfers or weekend warriors who have a life to contend with outside the golf course need drills that will enforce good habits and won't take up their golfing time. There are two putting drills that will do just that and only require 5 minutes of your time each time you go to play. Before you tee off, spend 10 minutes on the putting green, if you only have 5 minutes, spend 2 ½ minutes on each of these drills, you will be a better player for it and will leave the first tee in a good state of mind.

Putting Drill # 1, The Push Drill:

The Push Drill is the perfect way to get your putting stroke on track before the round. It's a very simple

Figure 76
With no back-swing, push the ball into the
hole and hold your finish position

drill that teaches acceleration, follow-through, putter path, and shoulder alignment. From 2-4 feet from the hole, take your set up and square yourself to the cup. Place the golf ball on your C.O.G. and your putter head directly behind the ball. With no back swing, simply push the ball into the hole and hold your finish position. Here's what to look for.

1) Is the ball rolling off the center of the putter face or is it rolling off the toe or the heel. If the ball is rolling off the toe of the putter face, your stroke is outside to in, if the ball is rolling off the heel, your stroke is inside to out. Simply check your set up and maintain your C.O.G. triangle, push a few more until the ball rolls off the center of the putter face.

2) Is the ball rolling off the center of the putter face but missing the hole or just catching the edge? This is a shoulder alignment problem; simply square your shoulders until the ball is going straight in the center of the hole. Within a few minutes, you will be making three footer after three footer using this drill and it seems to become hard to miss using this method. So much so, that I've been asked if it could be used on the golf course. Unfortunately, you can't use this on the course because the rules of golf state that we must fairly strike the golf ball, so the push is out. However the good news is that, when you set up to your putt on the golf course, you simply take a smooth backswing and push the putt toward the target. The confidence you get from making all those putts in a row will spill over on the golf course and you will make your share of short and mid range putts.

Putting Drill # 2, The LAG Drill:

The Lag Drill is designed to train you to see your target on long putts and use your eyes to gather all the information you need to get the ball close to the hole from a long distance. This drill will teach you how your eyes give the information to your brain so it can decide how hard you have to roll the putt in order to get the ball to the target. Your eyes are so good at gathering the information you need that, within a few putts, you will be rolling you lag putts up very close. Here's what you need to do.

1) Set up to a Lag Putt at 20-30 feet. Square up to the line of the putt and pick out a small target with your eyes and practice your stroke while looking at your target.

2) Set up to the ball and repeat your set-up procedure. Look at the ball to make sure your putter head is in the proper place and then look back to your target.

3) Make your stroke to the target, using your personal "pace" we worked out earlier while you're looking at the target. Don't take your eyes off your target when you stroke the ball - allow your eyes to judge the distance and tell your body how hard to stroke the ball.

You will be very surprised at how quickly you start to roll the ball close to the hole, even making a few. When you get to the golf course, make sure the last thing you see is your target and let your stroke go as soon as your eyes get back to the ball. This will ensure the last image your eyes see before the ball leaves the putter, is the target.

These two putting drills will improve your putting stats quickly and with minimal time investment. Use the 10-15 minutes before your tee time productively by finding your back toe/front toe distance, pushing in 10 or 15 putts in a row from 3 feet, and hitting some 20-50 foot lag putts while looking at your target. Your confidence will soar and your scores will come down.

The Putting Equation:

I don't believe good putters are born, I believe you can become a good putter with a little knowledge, a little practice, an understanding of the C.O.G. triangle, and the right attitude. Good putting requires these 3 things:

10% Physical Skill: You don't have to be an Olympic Athlete in order to be a good putter. In fact, some of the best putters in the world are kids and amateurs who love the challenge of beating some of the best Professionals in putting competitions by controlling their C.O.G., using imagination, and letting their stroke flow. For this reason, I believe anyone can become a good putter if they believe they can.

30% Imagination: Albert Einstein once said *"Imagination is more powerful than knowledge"*. Having a good imagination on the putting green will set you up to make more putts on a regular basis. When you get to the green, try to see the slope of the green by imagining how the water will drain off when it rains, or imagine the entire line of your putt from the ball to the hole and roll the ball on that line. Having a good imagination will help you "see" the

line and roll your putts with confidence. Having a good imagination does not mean taking all day walking around looking at a putt from all sides; in fact, if you use your first impression of how a putt breaks, you are probably right. Try to go with your first impression...you will be correct more often than not and make more putts on a regular basis.

Sandy Lane
"The Country Club"

Figure 77
All good putts don't necessarily go in

60% Confidence: The number one thing a good putter requires is confidence. A confident putter will roll the ball positively and will make more putts period. I know you had days on the golf course where you got to the first green, made a good putt, and you had a great day of putting where it seemed like everything was going in for you. Then there was the day you missed a couple of short putts early and you couldn't make anything all day. The result of both of those experiences was directly linked to your confidence level that day. It's imperative that you remain confident in your putting stroke and ability to make putts even when the first few stay out. Remember…there are a lot of things working against us on the putting green and all good putts don't necessarily go in.

16 "Putting your Game Together"

Now that you have an understanding of Center of Gravity Golf, its principles for consistency, and the simple breakdown of the different shots you need to execute in order to play this game, you can now break your game down into five components and focus on the ones that give you the most trouble. This way you can improve quickly by focusing on a specific part of your game instead of trying to do it all at once. Let's recap the 4 parts of the Center of Gravity golf game so you can begin to break them down, reduce your frustration, and lower your score.

Part 1) The Full Power 1...2...3...Swing:

The full power **1...2...3...** (Push, Engine, Piston) golf swing is designed to achieve maximum ball speed by separating the rotations of the swing, creating width and stability in the back swing, and firing the two rotations in the proper sequence. This swing will enhance ball flight and carry distance and give you distinct yardage differences between your irons. This is the swing you use for any full shot off the tee, in the fairway or rough, or when you need to advance the ball as far as you can with any given club.

The quickest way to re-program a poor swing sequence is to work out with a heavy golf club. A heavy golf club, in my opinion, is the best tool you could have in order to train your golf muscles as well as train (or re-train) a good 1...2...3...swing sequence. With your heavy club, practice your 3-piece golf swing in ¼ speed, exaggerating the separations of the golf swing making sure you turn the *Engine* before firing the *Piston*. After a week or so of swinging the heavy club in this way, you will have re-programmed your swing sequence.

Part 2) The Short Game 1...1...Swing:

The short shot producing **1...1...** *(Engine, Engine)* golf swing is designed to give you maximum control of your distances around the green. The 1...1... swing relies on your *Engine* to propel the golf ball eliminating the *Push* and the *Piston* from the swing. This will produce consistent short game distances that, when you use the "plan", will get the ball on the green and close to the hole from all your short game distances. This swing is used in the **Chipping Stroke** around the fringe of the green, in the **Finesse Shot** from 15 to 40 yards outside the green when you need a high soft shot to carry a hazard or to land soft on the green, and the **Greenside Bunker Shot** where you use the 1...1...shot to *"Turn"* the ball out of the bunker using your *Engine* as the power source. Learning how to execute this 1...1...golf swing with confidence will reduce your scores quickly and give you a short game you can count on.

Part 3) The "In Between" 1...2...Swing: (The Pitch Shot)

The **1...2...***(Engine, Piston)* golf swing produces those distances in between your 1...2...3...full swing and your 1...1...Short Game swing. By using your

1...1...(*Engine*, *Engine*) golf swing and **engaging your Piston** so it releases through the hitting zone, you create a series of pitching distances you can count on using the same basic move. By adding the *Piston* to the basic 1...1...golf swing, you can easily double your finesse distances and add those pitch shot distances to your short game shots.

Work on your 9 o'clock Finesse shot and add your *Piston*. You will soon see what your carry distance is and you can use it with confidence when you get into pitching distance. Now do the same with all the wedges in your bag as well as your 9, 8, and 7 irons. You'll be surprised at the shots you'll have at your disposal.

Part 4) The Putting Game:

The last piece of the puzzle in the C.O.G. method of playing and scoring is the putting game. The putting game requires you to have two qualities in order to succeed. The first quality is imagination, and the other is confidence. The putting set up and putting stroke are pretty straight forward as long as you are comfortable, and depend on you maintaining your **Center of Gravity Triangle** in order to become consistent.

Work on the two putting drills we spoke about in the putting section in order to build confidence in your putting stroke. The more confidence you have in your putting stroke, the more you can let your stroke flow, and the more putts you will make.

Success, Breeds Success:

Now that you have an understanding of what happens when you swing a golf club, you will notice that you will begin to have more success on the golf course and less miss hits. The more success you have, the more confident you become, and the more confident you become, the more success you have. Nothing builds confidence or breeds success like prior success. The **C.O.G.** swing method, short game system, and putting system are specifically designed to create success early and build on it to bring your game to a new level more quickly than ever.

It is my belief that learning to play golf, or improving your game doesn't have to be as complicated as you may think. *Center of Gravity Golf* will allow you to improve while freeing up your thoughts so you can focus on your target, instead of your swing mechanics.

Feeling vs. Seeing your golf swing:

I am not a huge believer in gadgets. There are so many superfluous, time wasting, money grubbing "products" out there for golfers to buy promising miracle cures for your slice, swing plane, leg drive, lag, you name it, someone has a product you can buy to fix it. I'm also not a great believer in video analysis, pro comparisons, computer angle and in swing data.

First of all, most gadgets are just that, gadgets you may use once with little or no success because you have no Professional feedback, advice, or guidance and, like most over the counter drugs, they are designed to treat a symptom, not the real problem.

A friend of mine was so excited to go to a PGA Tour teaching facility and pay an exorbitant amount of money to get hooked up to the motion capture computer analysis machine and wear the funny suit so they could examine his swing and putting stroke in 360 ° virtual reality. Long story short, he was so confused and overwhelmed with what he saw and tried to process that his golf game, and his attitude, suffered for his very expensive efforts. I had a similar scenario happen to me at a golf show in Los Angeles. This new golf technology company couldn't wait to show me how good their software was. They hooked a motion capture contraption to my putter and asked me to make a series of 6 foot putts. After making 4 of the 6 putts *(and narrowly missing the other 2 on the lip of the cup)* the salesman proudly exclaimed to everyone that my putter blade was ½ a degree open at impact and therefore should have his machine in order to correct it. Now maybe I'm not as smart as he is, or maybe I'm just old fashioned, but if I was to worry myself over ½ a degree in my putter blade at impact it would drive me crazy trying to make the adjustment.

Technology is a wonderful thing, and has its place in sports, even golf, but I've always believed that in any sport, especially golf, too much information is a very bad thing. A ½ degree variation in a putter blade at the point of impact could be the result of any one of a thousand things. Not only do I not want to deal with that personally, for $100.00 U.S. per session I will not subject my clients to such mental torture - I did not buy the technology.

There is no computer more powerful than your brain, and there is no software program smarter or more intuitive than your subconscious. Your subconscious can (and does) make dozens of minute changes during your golf swing to try to adapt to the conditions and decisions you've made and we should not try to override the program with conflicting information. *(Don't think so much!)*

I also believe to some degree the same goes with video teaching of the golf swing. I have concluded that video makes most students of the game, especially newcomers, very self conscious of how they look swinging a golf club. If their swing doesn't match the image of their favorite player or what they think is an esthetically pleasing golf swing they tie themselves up mentally and physically trying to change the image.

You can't see yourself swing a golf club, all you can do is "feel" what is going on in your muscles and body during the swing. You have to cultivate, capture, and remember what a good swing *feels* like...not what it looks like. I believe the golf swing should be felt, it should feel effortless and smooth, and it should produce the desired results - what else is there? A good golf swing should feel stable, smooth, powerful, effortless, and balanced.

Following the **Center of Gravity Golf** principles, you will soon feel what a golf swing should feel like. Starting with the **C.O.G.** triangle for stability and strength, the push away from the ball to feel the width of the swing and the power of the *Engine* priming to the top, the smooth transition of the *Engine* turning the golf swing back towards the ball, the powerful lag of the club head behind the turning *Engine*, the "butter like" feeling of compression as you fire your *Piston* through the bottom of your swing, and the stable, in balance finish position while you watch your golf ball soar.

Everybody's body works basically the same, however, most of us *(due to one thing or another)* have some physical limitations. Mine are left over from Hockey and Football, and therefore I can't hit the top of my backswing position that I used to. You must remember, the players you see on TV are professional athletes whose job it is to swing a golf club every day, so they're going to do it better than us, and it's very hard to emulate their movements. Find a Golf Professional who will work with your golf swing and physical limitations, then build a golf swing that feels great and works just as well.

Notes:

17 "Training for C.O.G."

Training Aids:

As I mentioned earlier, I'm not big on golf gadgets. Some of them might be fun for a few minutes and then they collect dust as you make you 3 easy payments of $39.95, but most of them aren't even fun. I do believe however, that everybody who is learning to swing a golf club, as well as seasoned players, should have a few things. Let's take a look.

1) A Weighted Club:

Every golfer should, in my opinion have a weighted golf club to swing a little on a daily basis. I think a weighted club is the very best golf training aid there is, and the good news is that you don't have to spend a fortune on one. A weighted golf club will help so many aspects of your game:

a) It will build your golf muscles.

b) Help to train the *Boss* fingers to control the club.

c) Encourages good balance and exposes balance flaws in your swing.

d) Works the important "core" muscles as your *Engine* pulls the weighted club through your swing.

e) It will ingrain very quickly the proper 1...2...3 golf swing sequence making sure you can feel the *Engine* pulling the golf club down from the transition zone (top of the swing).

f) Helps build power and stamina in your golf swing.

I use a weighted club every day to warm up and re-enforce proper swing motion and sequence - I even have one I can hit balls with. Now that's a good workout, and when I put my playing clubs in my hands they feel so light and move so fast, with very little effort. There are a few places you can get a weighted club, I have three that I work with depending on what I'm working on but I actually only purchased one.

Two of the clubs I'm speaking of I made, and so can you. There are always old clubs hanging around so I picked a couple that were still in pretty good shape and made my own training clubs. Down at the local hardware store I picked up a bottle of powdered lead, took the grips off the two 7 irons and filled one shaft about ½ full and the other I filled to the top. Plugged the shafts with some tape and epoxy resin (so the lead powder wouldn't slosh around) and had new grips installed on each club. I use these on a daily basis and they're going on 6 years old now. *Cost?* About $20.00 total for both.

The third weighted club I have I purchased at a golf retailer. I decided to get the *Momentus* weighted driver because you can actually safely hit balls with it. This is a tremendous tool as you not only get a great workout, but it's also a fantastic exercise in balance, rhythm, and sequence. There are a few choices out there for you in the weighted club department and I believe every golfer should have one…and use it.

2) A Squeeze Ball:

Every golfer, young or old should (*in my opinion*) have a soft ball they can squeeze from time to time while watching TV or walking. Residing in Canada, it's very easy for me to acquire my favorite squeezy toy, the sponge rubber hockey puck. It fits easily in my hand and is flat enough to put in my pocket when I'm done. Whatever you choose, these items are cheap and very effective. Squeeze balls and sponge rubber hockey pucks cost pennies and have many benefits:

a) Repetitive squeezing of a soft ball has been proven to reduce stress.

b) It will certainly strengthen your gripping power so your *"Boss fingers"* find it easy to control your golf club.

c) It will also strengthen your *Piston* so you can compress the golf ball more easily and hit it farther with more control.

Having a soft ball to squeeze on your down time is an effective and inexpensive way to quickly improve your control over your golf club.

3) A Large Exercise Ball:

The exercise ball is good for so many reasons. It works your stabilizing muscles, strengthens your core muscles, and improves your balance. All while giving you a great workout. If you want to hit the long ball, this is where it counts.

Power in the golf swing does not come from the legs, or arms, it comes from your core. The core muscles of your abdomen produce the torque to swing the golf club fast. The Core muscles are the "*Engine*" of your golf swing and therefore require attention. Not convinced? Check out the core on 5 time world long drive champion Jason Zubak some time. I've witnessed Jason fly a golf ball over 450 yards, and I had a glimpse at his training ball workout. We all can't work out as long or hard as Jason but the fact is, if you want to be long, make your core strong. Not to mention all of the other benefits you'll enjoy.

4) Yoga or Stretching Program:

A good daily stretching program will be the best thing you can do for your golf game and your body. There are a few golf specific golf yoga programs available that offer beginner, intermediate and advanced sessions to make sure everyone can participate and improve flexibility while enhancing their golf swing as well as their daily quality of life.

A well designed stretching and breathing program

will increase your range of motion, prevent injuries, and allow your body to execute the proper golf swing sequence effortlessly and with graceful power.

Everything I've mentioned above is readily available, inexpensive, and highly effective in quickly improving your swing mechanics, strength, balance, and focus on the golf course. Always beware of the *"Miracle Gadget"* - I've seen Golf Pros with kit bags full of this stuff and as with most things in life, the simplest things are the best.

Teaching the golf swing has been a passion of mine for a long time. The satisfaction I feel when a golfer "gets it" is tremendous to say the least. I wish you rapid success and big smiles every day on the golf course.

Rob Bernard CPGA

Glossary of Terms

1) **C.O.G.** – Refers to "Center of Gravity" as it relates to the golf swing.

2) **ENGINE** – Refers to the rotation of the body during the golf swing

3) **PISTON** – Refers to the release of the club-head during the golf swing.

4) **CNS** – Refers to your Central Nervous System

5) **The 1 -1 Swing** – Refers to the swing motion using only the "*Engine*"

6) **The 1 – 2 Swing** – Refers to the swing motion using the "*Engine*" & "*Piston*" motion only.

7) **The 1-2-3-Swing** – Refers to the swing motion utilizing all 3 parts of the golf swing the "*Push*", "*Engine*", & "*Piston*"

"Rob is an excellent, inspirational instructor and speaker, his seminars were clear, concise and always a BIG HIT with our clients, Rob fills the room & keeps them there!"
- Paul Hancox - Cruise Director, Princess Cruise Lines

"Rob Bernard not only has something to say, but backs it up with probably the most innovative approach to the game of golf I've witnessed in my 40 years of playing. I recommend his presentation to anyone who is looking for improvement not only in golf, but in life as well. Rob will keep your audience enthralled!"
- Steve Moris - Comedian/Musician, The Beach Boys

"Rob Bernard is a talented and dynamic speaker who has created a unique golf system that he uses to motivate his listeners in an extremely fascinating, informative and entertaining manner. He makes you want to grab your clubs and hit the course with a re-born confidence and enthusiasm."
- Phil Egan - Publisher, Within 2 Hours Magazine

"He immediately connected with me and the audience; I couldn't believe how strong the positive feedback was ".
- Darryl Branstetter – Guthy-Renker Corporation

To book a Live Golf Seminar series or Private or Corporate Clinics with Rob, visit the Seminar and Clinic section of the website at
WWW.COGOLF.CA

LaVergne, TN USA
13 January 2010
169932LV00002B/40/P